Happy Christmas and
happy fishing.

All love,
Bill & Eileen '90.

The Best Fishing in Scotland

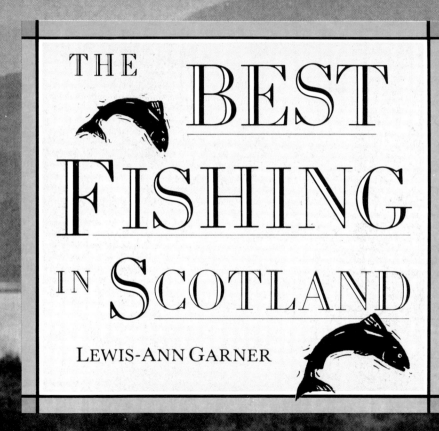

THE BEST FISHING IN SCOTLAND

LEWIS-ANN GARNER

©Lewis-Ann Garner 1990

Published by
Lochar Publishing Ltd
MOFFAT DG10 9JU

Designed by Hammond Hammond

British Library Cataloguing in Publication Data
Garner, Lewis-Ann
    The best fishing in Scotland.
    1. Scotland. Angling
    I. Title
    799.1209411

ISBN 0-948403-29-2

Typeset in Plantin by Chapterhouse,
The Cloisters, Formby, L37 3PX
Printed and bound in Great Britain by
Butler & Tanner Ltd, Frome and London

Picture Credits
Shetland p. 51, Orkney fisherman p. 55 – Shetland Tourist
Organisation.

Loch of Harray p. 49, River Don p. 91, Island of Harris p. 101,
p. 108, Loch Eilt p. 123, Loch Watten p. 127, p. 129,
Gladhouse Reservoir p. 134 – B M Sandison.

For Michael
'the mome raths outgrabe'

Introduction

This is a book about gamefishing in Scotland. It does not pretend to be a definitive description of Scottish sport, but I hope that it may help you find the sort of fishing that suits you best.

The rivers and lochs detailed offer, in my opinion, some of the best scottish angling; should my views differ from your own, then I apologise: one man's dream is sometimes another man's nightmare – or, in this case, a woman's. Much of the fishing is beyond the price range of average anglers. Nevertheless, it is always worth enquiring from estates and owners to see whether or not the occasional rod may be available.

The key to a successful gamefishing holiday in Scotland is careful pre-planning and early booking. Much of the best fishing is booked well in advance and to have any chance of obtaining access to many waters, you may well have to plan several years ahead.

My thanks are due to my publisher, Michael De Luca, for giving me the opportunity to write this guide (and for his patience and encouragement). I must fully acknowledge my gratitude to my father, Bruce Sandison who has given me the benefit of his support and advice in the preparation of this book. And to my husband for his wonderful photographs. He travelled several hundred miles throughout Scotland, falling victim to all weather conditions – blizzards in the Cairngorms; damp, misty dawns beside Loch Tay; watery sunsets on the Border Esk; and, I believe, the occasional warm and sunny day. He battled against them all, clutching camera and tripod. But now he has put these aside. His next attack on Scotland will be with rod, creel and hip-flask.

Finally, I must thank the rest of my family and my friends for their support and help in making this book possible. I wish them all, and the reader, a fish or three for the glass-case.

Lewis-Ann Garner.

LEWIS-ANN GARNER
(January, 1990)

Contents

1. The Tweed and its Tributaries

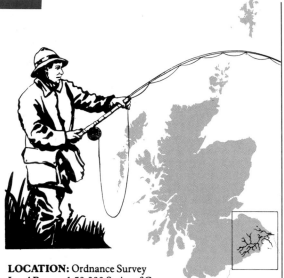

LOCATION: Ordnance Survey
Land Ranger 1:50,000 Series of Great
Britain. Sheets 78, Nithsdale and
Lowther Hills; 72, Upper Clyde Valley; 73, Galashiels and
Ettrick Forest; 79, Hawick and Eskdale; 80, The Cheviot
Hills; 74, Kelso; 67, Duns and Dunbar; and 75, Berwick-
upon-Tweed.

GRID REFERENCES: Sheet 78, Tweed's Well, 055145.
Sheet 72, Tweedsmuir, 095245; Drumelzier Water, 134354;
Stobo, 184375. **Sheet 73,** Manor Junction, 229395; Peebles
246404; Innerleithen, 335365; Traquair House, 332354;
Walkerburn, 362371; Ettrick-Yarrow junction, 444274;
Ettrick-Tweed junction, 485323; Pavillion Water, 545345.
Sheet 74, Leader-Tweed junction, 577346; Makerstoun
Water, 670314; Teviot-Tweed junction, 724338; Teviot-Ale
junction, 629235; Hendersyde Water, 746353; Carham Water,

804390; Coldstream, 843397; Till-Tweed junction, 870430;
Tillmouth Park, 885427; Ladykirk House, 887458;
Whiteadder-Blackadder junction, 864545. **Sheet 75,**
Whiteadder-Tweed junction, 973517.

SEASONS: Salmon – February 1–November 30. Upper
reaches of Tweed and some beats begin fishing later in the
season, and some offer sport only during autumn months.
Check before you go. Best months are October and November.
Trout – April 1–September 30. Some of the tributaries offer
earlier trout fishing, but fish are seldom in peak condition.
Best months are late May, June and July.

FLIES: Salmon – Garry Dog, Silver Doctor, Silver
Wilkinson, Thunder and Lightening, Willie Gunn, Blue
Doctor. Trout – Blue Dun, March Brown, Black Spider,
Greenwell's Glory, Peter Ross.

COSTS: Excellent brown-trout fishing can be had for the day
anywhere on Tweed for less than £10; some is as cheap as £1
for the entire season.
   The cost of salmon and sea-trout fishings varies. Upper
Tweed, around Peebles, will cost from £20 to £50 for five days,
depending on the time of season. In the Walkerburn area, a
week's fishing will cost from £72 to £311 per beat. Anglers can
expect to pay between £86.25 and £115 to fish Boleside beat.
Guests staying at Tillmouth Hotel will pay £50–£80 per day
or £275–£475 per week per rod. These prices include a boat
and the services of a gillie. Book well in advance whenever
possible, be prepared for years of waiting to get on to some
beats. A day on one of Tweed's famous beats is well worth it.
   The Scottish Borders Tourist Board, Municipal Buildings,
High Street, Selkirk (Tel: 0750–2055), will advise non-fishing
visitors on where to go and what to see.

PERMISSION: Upper Tweed: The Crook Inn,
Tweedsmuir, Peeblesshire (Tel: 08997–272).
Peebles: Peeblesshire Trout Fishing Association, D G Fyfe,
39, High Street, Peebles (Tel: 0721–20131).

Peebles and various beats downstream: Ian Fraser
Sports, 1 Bridgegate, Peebles (Tel: 0721–20979).
Peebles: Peeblesshire Salmon Fishing Association, Messrs
Blackwood & Smith, 39 High Street, Peebles (Tel:
0721–20131).
Peebles and various beats downstream: Tweed Valley
Hotel, Walkerburn, Peeblesshire (Tel: 089687–220).
Kailzie Water: Mrs M A Richard, Kailzie, by Peebles (Tel:
0721–20007).
Traquair Water: Traquair Arms Hotel, Innerleithen,
Peeblesshire (Tel: 0896830–229).
Sunderland Hall: Mr R Smyly, Sunderland Hall,
Galashiels, Selkirkshire (Tel: 0750–20979).
Galashiels: Gala Angling Association, J & A Turnbull, 30
Bank Street, Galashiels, Selkirkshire (Tel: 0896–3191).
Galashiels: Clovenford Hotel, Clovenfords, Galashiels,
Selkirkshire (Tel: 089685–203).
Galashiels: Thornilee Hotel, Clovenfords by Galashiels,
Selkirkshire (Tel: 08965–350).
Melrose: Anglers' Choice, High Street, Melrose,
Roxburghshire (Tel: 089682–3070).
St Boswell's: St Boswell's Angling Association, Q McLaren,
Rowansbrae, Tweedside Road, Newton St Boswell's,
Roxburghshire.
Dryburgh Water: Dryburgh Abbey Hotel, St Boswell's,
Roxburghshire (Tel: 0835–22261).
Mertoun and Makerstoun Waters: Bell Ingram Limited, 7
Walker Street, Edinburgh (Tel: 031225–3271).
Kelso: Kelso Angling Association, J Dickson & Sons, 35 The
Square, Kelso, Roxburghshire (Tel: 0573–24687).
Kelso: Game Fair, 12 Marygate, Berwick-upon-Tweed (Tel:
0289–305119).
Hendersyde and other Tweed beats: J H Leeming,
Chartered Surveyor, Stichil House, Kelso, Roxburghshire
(Tel: 05737–288).
Birgham Water: The Hon Caroline Douglas-Home,
Douglas and Angus Estate, The Hirsel, Coldstream,
Berwickshire.

RIVER TWEED. Anglers at Norham make the final casts of the day in the hope of catching a late returning salmon. The record British sea-trout, 28 lb 9 oz, was taken from the waters at Norham, unfortunately it was netted.

Cornhill Water: Tillmouth Park Hotel, Cornhill-on-Tweed, Northumberland (Tel: 0890–2255).

Twizel Water, Tweed and Till: Game Fair, 12 Marygate, Berwick-upon-Tweed (Tel: 0289–305119).

Milne Water: The Manager, Milne Garden, Coldstream, Berwickshire (Tel: 0289–82245).

Ladykirk: Mason's Arms, Norham, Berwick-upon-Tweed (Tel: 0289–82326).

Lyne Water: I Fraser, Northgate, Peebles (Tel: 0721–20979).

Lyne Water: Tweed Valley Hotel, Walkerburn, Peebleshire (Tel: 089687–220).

Ettrick, Yarrow and Teviot: The Factor, The Buccleuch Estate Limited, Bowhill, Selkirk (Tel: 0750–20753).

Ettrick and Teviot: The Buccleuch Arms Hotel, St Boswell's, Roxburghshire (Tel: 0835–22243).

Ettrick: Robert Smyly, Sunderland Hall, Galashiels, Selkirkshire (Tel: 0750–21298).

Ettrick: Ettrickshaws Hotel, Ettrick Bridge, Selkirkshire (Tel: 0750–52229).

Gala Water: Gala Angling Association, S Grybowski, 3 St Andrew's Street, Galashiels, Selkirkshire.

Leader Water: Earlston Angling Association, P Hessett, 2 Arnott Place, Earlston, Berwickshire (Tel: 089684–577).

Jed Water: Jedforest Country House Hotel, Camptown, Roxburghshire (Tel: 08354–274).

Kale Water: Mr Graham, Eckford Cottage, Eckford, Kelso, Roxburghshire (Tel: 08355–255).

Teviot: Miss S Scott, Lothian Estate Office, Jedburgh, Roxburghshire (Tel: 0835–62201).

Teviot and Ale Water: Stothart's, Tackle Shop, 6 High Street, Hawick, Roxburghshire (Tel: 0450–72234).

Teviot and Eden Water: Redpath & Co, Horsemarket, Kelso, Roxburghshire (Tel: 0573–24578).

Eden Water: J H Fairgrieve, Burnbank, Gordon, Berwickshire (Tel: 057381–357).

Leet Water: Coldstream Angling Association, Tweed Fishing Tackle, Market Street, Coldstream, Berwickshire.

Till: Tillmouth Park Hotel, Cornhill-on-Tweed, Coldstream, Berwickshire (Tel: 0890–2255).

Whiteadder Water: Whiteadder Angling Association, J Boyd, St Leonard's, Polwarth, Duns, Berwickshire (Tel: 0361–82377).

Blackadder Water: Greenlaw Angling Club, J Purves, 9 Wester Row, Greenlaw, Berwickshire.

TWEED IS A gentle giant among Scottish salmon rivers. Waters flow from rugged moorlands through sweeping valleys of woodland and fertile pasture before spilling into the North Sea. Year after year Tweed gives anglers salmon, trout, and sea-trout of glass case size. Its biggest salmon, caught in 1730, weighed 69 lb 12 oz. In 1983, G Leavy caught a beautiful 20 lb sea-trout, the rod-caught record for the river.

Salmon are caught mainly on the famous beats between Kelso and Coldstream. Here, the wide, deep pools can be fished even when the rest of Tweed is low. Some Tweed pools are more than 30 ft deep, but boat fishing allows even the biggest and deepest of the lower pools to be covered completely. Try always to employ a gillie; if fish are about, his knowledge will help you have a day to remember.

Tweed begins its long journey deep in Dumfriesshire, a few miles north of Moffat, where the famous Tweed's Well is marked by a sign next to the road. Little bubbling burns tumble down from Foal Burn Head (509 m) and Flecket Hill (463 m) to flow northwards, but the real source of Tweed lies amid the rough sedges and purple heather of the bleak moorland. Soon, these run through dark-green forestry plantations, land which once was bog, clumped with rushes and dotted with silver-headed cotton grass.

At the foot of Badenhay Rig (454 m), Tweed is joined by Carr Water, which cascades from its source next to the haunting chasm of the Devil's Beef Tub. It is from near here, too, that the Annan begins its southerly journey to the Solway.

Carr Water splashes into Tweed and hurries it along to Tweedhopefoot to meet with its next tributary, Tweedhope Burn. A mile further on,

Tweed receives the peaty waters of Glencraigie Burn, racing from the boggy moorlands of Falla Moss (485 m).

The first bridge across Tweed is at Fingland, on the edge of Tweedsmuir, and it is below this that Tweed finally shakes off the conifers which have hidden its sparkling waters. During the next 13 miles the main stream is joined by many cascading burns, all springing from sources on the empty moorlands, the haunt of grouse, curlew and little owl. The burn margins are studded with emerald mosses and clumped with golden bracken, Talla and Fruid waters, have been dammed to provide water for Edinburgh. Talla Water joins Tweed just below Tweedsmuir's sprawling village. It was around here that John Buchan roamed as a child, walking the surrounding valley and stalking elusive brown trout.

AN EASTERLY COURSE

As Biggar and Holms water flow into Tweed below Merlindale, so the river turns east. The fiery moorlands are gradually left behind and banks of Tweed are graced with parklands and buttercup meadows.

The next tributary to join Tweed is Lyne Water, which once flowed freely from the long curve of the heather-covered Pentland Hills. Now its waters are trapped to form Baddinsgill Reservoir, but the river still offers wonderful brown-trout fishing.

Before reaching Peebles, Tweed is met by sweet-flowing Manor Water, racing north from the steep slopes of Shielhope Head (613 m). Manor Water is a swirling, peaty river, flowing through rough moorland before its final stretches

wash over smoothed stones, beneath a canopy of beech, oak, ash and willow. Close by Tweed stands Neidpath Castle, its walls still pockmarked by Cromwell's cannonballs.

Historic Peebles is where Tweed's salmon and sea-trout fishing really begins. Above the town fishing is mainly for wild brown trout; salmon seldom reach so far upstream until late summer. Indeed, some Upper Tweed beats are fished only from October 1 until November 30, the closing day for the whole river. Peebles' beautiful bridge dates from the mid-fifteenth century spanning the water with five glorious arches.

Tweed flows swiftly from Peebles, skirting Kailzie Gardens and the thick conifers of Cardrona Forest, and then passing through gentle pastures and steeply wooded hills. Beats along this stretch are Peebles Burgh water, Haystoun, Horsburgh Castle, Kailzie, Nether Horsburgh, Cardrona and Traquair.

On Traquair, Tweed is joined by Quair Water as it tumbles by ancient Traquair House, the oldest occupied Scottish home. It belongs to the Maxwell Stuarts, and parts of it date back to 1107 AD. On the estate are The Bear Gates, which, legend says will never be opened again until a Stuart is once more on the throne. Traquair Water produces an average of more than 70 salmon each season. Trout fishing on the tributary Leithen Water is available to visiting anglers, the brown trout averaging around 6 oz.

Innerleithen, on this stretch of Tweed, is famous for its textile manufacturing. Its adopted patron saint is St Ronan, and people used to come to drink from a spring on the hillside, believing the water to have healing properties. The saint and the well are together immortalised in Sir

RIVER TWEED. The most famous pool on Tweed is the Junction Pool where Tweed gathers in the waters of the River Teviot. A weeks fishing for five rods in this pool will cost anglers in the region of £17,000.

Walter Scott's novel, *St Ronan's Well*, published in 1824.

Tweed flows briskly from Innerleithen, its banks spoiled by sprawling conifer plantations, but passing through the Pirn, Caberstoun, Holylee, Elbibank, Thornilee, Ashiesteel, Peel, Caddonlee, Caddonfoot, Yair, Fairnilee, Boleside and Sunderland beats. The heaviest salmon in recent years from Upper Tweed was a 29½-pounder taken in the Wirebridge Pool on Kingsmeadow by Bill Doidge.

It is on the last two stretches that Tweed is joined by its first major tributary, Ettrick Water This wide, sweeping river begins faraway on the edge of Eskdalemuir Forest, not far from Moffat. It is an excellent salmon river and has a good spawning run. It also provides good brown-trout fishings, as does its own large tributary, Yarrow Water. The trout run at 8–12 oz, and fish of more than 3 lb are not uncommon.

A WEALTH OF TRIBUTARIES

Yarrow Water flows through rough grasslands and heather moors before splashing by the ruins of Newark Castle and winding its way to meet with Ettrick Water at Philiphaugh. In the triangle between the junctions is Bowhill, Borders home of the Duke of Buccleuch.

From here, Ettrick flows to Selkirk town, about a mile further north. This historic Scottish town has three famous statues. In market square is one to Sir Walter Scott, most famous of all Scottish writers. The second is in memory of Mungo Park, a local man who discovered the source of the River Niger in Africa during the late 1700s. But the third is perhaps the saddest, to a man called Fletcher, the only one of 80 soldiers

Notable Tweed salmon caught in recent years

1987–1989

WEIGHT	ANGLER	LOCATION	WEIGHT	ANGLER	LOCATION
40 lb 8 oz	K Beattie	Bemersyde	21 lb	Mr Scott	Rutherford
35 lb	P Brett	Tillmouth Park	20 lb	Mr Hewitt	Carham
33 lb	E Gregory	The Lees	20 lb	M Rigby	Junction
29 lb 8 oz	W Doidge	Kingsmeadow	19 lb	F Tyson	Rutherford
27 lb 8 oz	D Simpson	Junction	19 lb	D Walker	Mertoun
27 lb	Mr Blackhurst	Sprouston	18 lb	Mrs Watson	Sprouston
27 lb	H Falkus	Junction	18 lb	A Richardson	Traquair
27 lb	A Robinson	Hendersyde	18 lb	D J Evans	Carham
26 lb 8 oz	B Hanson	Carham	17 lb 8 oz	I Merrill	North Wark
26 lb	Mr Baker	Dryburgh	17 lb	Sir C Lever	Rutherford
26 lb	G Curry	Lower Birgham	17 lb	P Rogers	Mertoun
26 lb	C Millar	Junction	17 lb	G Green	South Wark
26 lb	M and J Green	Glenmoriston			
26 lb	A Usher	Lower Mertoun			
25 lb	M Cox	Makerstoun			
25 lb	Miss J Lovat	Wark			
25 lb	A Worswick	Mertoun			
25 lb	H Barker	Tillmouth			
25 lb	Mr Thompson	Rutherford			
25 lb	Mr Mann	Lower Makerstoun			
25 lb	W Burns	Hendersyde			
24 lb	Sir J Hogg	Glenmoriston			
24 lb	Sir N Stockdale	Hendersyde			
24 lb	Mrs Hughes	Birgham Dub			
24 lb	Duchess of Sutherland	Middle Mertoun			
23 lb	Mrs Blackhurst	Sprouston			
23 lb	Mr Sparks	Lower Birgham			
23 lb	Mr Mellor	Sprouston			
22 lb	Cdr M Atkinson	Mertoun			

from Selkirk to return from the Battle of Flodden in September, 1513. When he entered the town, he cast down the English Standard he had captured and wept with despair. Not only had the battle seen the defeat of the Scots, but the death of their king, James IV. Every year an enactment of the 'Casting of the Colours' takes place in memory of those fallen.

Boleside Water, on the opposite bank from Sunderland Water, where Ettrick Water joins Tweed, gave anglers 181 salmon, two grilse and 17 sea-trout in October, 1989. The average weight of the salmon was 10 lb, although some of more than 20 lb were taken.

From here Waters of Tweed are Upper, Middle and Lower Pavillion, Drygrange, Old Melrose, Gledswood, Ravenswood, Bemersyde, Drybergh, Maxton, Merton, Rutherford, Makerstoun and Upper and Lower Floors, at the lower end of which the Teviot spills its waters into Tweed in the famous Junction Pool at Kelso.

HISTORIC CONNECTIONS

The next tributary to swell Tweed is Gala Water, which flows from the slopes of the Moorfoot Hills south along a narrow valley floor to meet Tweed below Galashiels Town. Brown-trout fishing on Gala Water and 12 miles of Tweed around here are controlled by Galashiels Angling Association.

From here, Tweed flows on to collect the Allan Water before flowing through Melrose town at the foot of the Eildon Hills. It is reputed that the heart of Robert Bruce lies buried in the ruins of its Cistercian Abbey, dating from the twelfth century. Overlooking the town, on Eildon Hills, are remains of a 1,900-year-old Roman fort, from which the guards had a clear view of Dere Street, the main England–Scotland road.

Downstream from Melrose, Tweed is met by Leader Water at Leaderfoot. Brown-trout fishing can provide wonderful sport, with fish averaging 8 oz, and with bigger specimens being taken occasionally. Leader Water splashes from the north, its waters rendering Tweed red and unfishable in times of heavy rain.

Leader Water's course is closely followed by the busy A68 as its journey to Tweed takes it past beautiful Thirlestane Castle, its sandstone walls glowing pink under the summer sun. Thirlestone's east wing is home to the Border Country Life Museum. The Maitland family, to whom the castle is still home, once had an ancestor rule Scotland for Charles II.

On Bemersyde Hill (228 m), overlooking Gledswood Water, is Scott's view. Stretched out below are red-soil pasturelands with field boundaries of lime, beech, thorn and oak as Tweed rolls gracefully by, its waters shimmering in the sunshine. This was Scott's favourite view in his beloved Border country. An angler's favourite view around here might be less expansive. Mr K Beattie's was undoubtedly Cromweil Pool Bemersyde Beat, where he caught a 40½ lb salmon while he was boat fishing there in the shadow of the growing hill.

Next town on Tweed's banks is St Boswell's, with its abbey built by monks from Alnwick in Northumbria in 1150 AD. This is the final resting place of both Sir Walter Scott and Field-Marshall Earl Haig, Commander-in-Chief of British Forces on the Western Front from 1915–1918.

Two tributaries join Tweed along here, the Bogle Burn and West Burn. The Bogle flows from the slopes of the three Eildon Hills, in the heart of which, legend says, sleeps King Arthur and the Knights of the Round Table. West Burn comes from windswept White Law Hill (323 m).

These stretches of Tweed are all liable to flooding as the river flows from long, dark pools into swift, splashing rapids, its waters lapping on shingle and around wooded islands. The farmlands bordering Tweed from here down are some of the best in Scotland, their red sandstone soils rich in minerals.

From where Leader Water joins begins what is regarded by many as the best salmon fishing in the world. It is also some of the most expensive and most sought-after. Upper and Lower Floors Waters yielded 584 and 330 salmon respectively in 1988, and the five-year average for October fishing on these two beats is 160 and 130 salmon.

CHANGING FORTUNES

One-hundred-and-thirty-six years after Earl Home landed his legendary 69 lb 12 oz salmon, Mr Pryor, fishing Floors Water at Kelso, landed a 57 lb 8 oz salmon. This fish is regarded by many as the biggest Tweed fish, and no other fish approaching this weight has been taken since it was caught in 1886. Nowadays, Tweed salmon are likely to be 10–12 lb, although 30-pounders are still there to be caught on occasion.

One reason for the decline in weighty fish is coastal and river netting. The biggest sea-trout taken from Tweed, at Norham, was netted. It weighed 28 lb 9 oz, and remains the largest sea-trout ever taken from British waters. How much nicer it would have been if an angler could have won this magnificent fish from Tweed.

With netting rights bought-out all along the

river, the improvement in sea-trout fishing has been considerable. Tweed has always been famed for these fish, which although few in number, more than compensate with their size. September, 1989, saw four taken by guests of Tillmouth Hotel, fishing Twizel Waters. These averaged over 6 lb. Tweed will be a sea-trout river to be reckoned with in the future.

At Kelso, where Teviot floods into Tweed, lies, perhaps, the most famous pool of the river: The Junction. A week's fishing here for five rods at prime time costs £17,000, yet it is booked for years in advance.

The Teviot with its source in the fringes of Eskdalemuir Forest, is a salmon and sea-trout water in its own right. Noted pools are Quarry, Lower and Ferry Stream. All have given salmon of more than 20 lb. Its principal tributaries are Bothwick Water, which joins at the foot of Branzholmpark Hill (250 m), and Lang Burn, which mingles with the main stream at Hawick.

Overlooking Teviotdale is a column built to honour the Duke of Wellington. Erected in 1815, it stands on Peniel Haugh (237 m), from where it is possible to see the bright waters of the Ale flowing east to join with Teviot at Ancrum. Caves along its banks are said to have been used by fugitives during the long and turbulent Border Wars.

Also visible from the column is the golden thread of Jed Water, which rises in Wauchope Forest, high in the rolling Cheviots. The Jed flows through historic Jedburgh, with its Abbey founded in 1138 by King David I, but now a beautiful ruin. The sixteenth-century castle house, now a museum, is where Queen Mary of Scotland spent some time in 1566, before her imprisonment in England.

As Jed Water washes northwards out of Jedburgh, it flows past a high, fiery-red sandstone bank, its innumerable layers of sedimentary rock exposed to wind, water and sun by the action of the water over thousands of years. Downstream, Jed Water splashes into Teviot at the edge of Monteviot House gardens, and then its waters considerably swollen, tumbles along to gather in Kale Water before itself being embraced by Tweed.

From the Junction Pool at Kelso to Tweed's confluence with the Till are some famous salmon beats: Hendersyde, Sprouston, Birgham, Carham, Lower Birgham, Wark, Wark Temple, Cornhill, Lennel and Twizel. Hendersyde and Sprouston saw more then 600 salmon taken during September and October 1989. Birgham, next door is where Mr Rudd landed a 50 lb 8 oz salmon in 1925. Wark had more than 120 fish for October, 1989.

Tweed's best runs of salmon, and the biggest fish, come now in autumn, preceded, during summer, by good runs of grilse averaging about 6 lb. Spring fishing used to be excellent, but now few springers are about and the fish that do come are only 6–8 lb. The best brown-trout fishing is from June to August. One angler, J Colin, landed a 7 lb 12 oz trout from Makerstoun not long ago.

QUIET RETREATS

Parts of Tweed do become rather crowded with anglers; if you want solitude, then try the tributaries. You may not catch a glass-case specimen, but the river will be yours for a day.

As Tweed mixes with Eden Water, so it becomes the boundary between Scotland and England. Half of Tweed is in Scotland, half in England. The Eden itself is a charming trout stream.

The Till, a salmon and sea-trout water in its own right, flows into Tweed on Twizel water. It comes together from many burns cascading from the Cheviot Hills, but first as the Breamish. Not until it flows past Chillingham Park, famous for its wild white cattle, does it became the Till.

North of Wooler, Till is joined by the Glen, which also rises in the Cheviots. Its course now is through a gentle countryside of deciduous woodlands and rolling pasture to the Tweed.

Downstream from Till junction, Tweed meanders from deep pool to wide rapids, streaming round the many islands, taking in the famous beats of Ladykirk and Norham. Last year (1989) a three-and-a-half-mile stretch of single-bank fishing at Ladykirk came on to the market at an asking price of £800,000. Ladykirk accounted for 71 salmon and 12 sea-trout in October, 1989, a figure which no doubt will be surpassed now that the nets are off.

Norham stands across the river from Ladykirk. It was here that the 28½ lb sea-trout mentioned earlier was netted. Norham Castle visible from the river, once had so bad a reputation that Sir Walter Scott dubbed it the most dangerous place to be in England. He immortalised the castle, built in 1157 and witness to many battles and skirmishes during the Border Wars, in his poem, *Marmion*.

It was at Norham that the Blessing of the Nets ceremony used to be held. Tradition was that the vicar was always given the first fish. Now, rod-anglers' prayers have been answered and the nets have been taken off.

Downstream again, about a mile east of Paxton House and upstream of the confluence of the Whiteadder, the Scottish-English Border cuts north across Tweed. The river's last few miles lie entirely through England.

The Whiteadder is Tweed's last tributary. It flows south over the Border from burns tumbling together from the green-and-purple Lammermuir Hills. Its upper reaches, above Cranshaws, have been dammed and flooded, to provide water for Edinburgh. Lower down, the Whiteadder Angling Association has restocked with brown and rainbow trout.

The two largest tributaries of Whiteadder are Dye Water and Blackadder. Watchwater, a tributary of Dye, has also been dammed for water-supply purposes. The Blackadder meets the river at Allanton. Together, these burns offer the trout angler a wonderful opportunity to take a short, light rod to fish amid the beautiful unspoiled Lammermuirs.

From Whiteadder junction, Tweed is affected by tides, ebbing and flowing over a mixture of shifting sands and mud until, at last, its waters glide under the majestic old Royal Border Bridge, swirl past Tweedmouth and are lost in the North Sea. It is, unless a winter nor'-easter is blowing a silent end to a mighty river.

RIVER TWEED. South from Melrose at Gattonside. This stretch of Tweed flows through beautiful woodlands and gentle lowland pastures. Brown trout fishing in this area is excellent.

2. Sutherland

S UTHERLAND IS ONE
of the most dramatic and
varied counties in Scotland. In the east, sweeping
from the slopes of Ben Loyal to the flat Caithness
plains, lies the Flow Country: thousands of acres
of sphagnum moss, jewelled by bog asphodel,
spotted orchid, milkwort and bog myrtle, and
bobbed white with cotton grass.

Red-throated divers float serenely on remote
lochans; hen harriers and golden eagles lord the
skies; otters and wild cats hunt through the
wilderness; and red deer haughtily mark an
intruder's slow and stumbling progress across the
flows. It is a landscape that has lain undisturbed
by the hand of man for thousands of years.

West of the Flow Country rises Sutherland's
wild array of magnificent mountains: Foinaven
and the grey screes of Arkle; shapely Ben Stack,
guarding Loch Stack; Ben Hope, shadowing its
own loch; Quinaig, the spout, by windy Loch
Assynt; Suilven, Canisp and mighty Ben More
Assynt, Sutherland's highest peak.

Gracing this scenic wonderland is some of
Scotland's finest gamefishing. Its salmon streams
have magic in their names: Naver, Helmsdale,
Halladale, Dionard, Inver and Kirkaig; its sea-
trout lochs, Hope and Stack are superb; and some
of the best wild brown trout fishing to be found
anywhere can be had in the Durness lochs,
Caladail, Borralie, Lanlish and Croispol.

T WO GILLIES outside
the hotel at Altna-
hara in Sutherland are
ready and waiting for
their gentleman. The
knowledge of the gillie
can mean the difference
between a week to
remember and a holiday
best forgotten.

RIVER TWEED. The confluence of the Tweed with the River Till. A weeks salmon fishing on this stretch, Twizel Water, will cost, at prime times, over £470 per rod. This includes the use of a boat and the services of a gillie.

RIVER TWEED. Best salmon and sea-trout fishing on Tweed begins at Peebles. A few miles downstream an angler who hopes that his prayers will be answered and that he will finish the day with a Tweed salmon.

LOCH STACK. One of the most beautiful lochs in Scotland. It offers anglers the chance to catch wild brown trout, silver salmon or sea-trout. The excellence of sea-trout fishing is prized. Book well in advance.

RIVER OYKEL. To be sure of a day on the river anglers should book at least a year in advance. Upwards of 1,500 salmon are taken each year and at the close of the 1989 season over 2,000 had been caught. Prospects for 1990 are looking even better.

The Halladale

LOCATION: Ordnance Survey Second Series 1:50,000. Sheet 10, Strathnaver.

GRID REFERENCES: Melvich, 880650; Trantlemore, 892532; Forsinard Hotel, 891426.

SEASON: Salmon – February 10–September 30.

FLIES: Stoat's Tail, Willie Gunn, Shrimp Fly, Garry Dog, Munro Killer, Waddingtons.

COSTS: Weekly, on Lower Halladale, from £100 £400, depending upon time of year; day-tickets are sometimes available from £25. Upper Halladale is available for Forsinard Hotel residents at £7.50 per day; non-residents' tickets may be available at £15 per day.

PERMISSION: Lower Halladale from Mrs J Atkinson, 8 Sinclair Street, Thurso, Caithness (Tel: 0847–63291). Upper Halladale from Forsinard Hotel, Forsinard, Strath Halladale, Sutherland (Tel: 06417–221).

R IVER HALLADALE. This river is very dependent on rainfall to keep it fishable during summer months. With the netting in Melvich Bay now halted the seasonal average of 150 salmon is expected to

T HE HALLADALE RIVER, in the east of the county, has excellent runs of spring salmon which average 8 lb, although best sport is had during autumn. Upwards of 150 salmon are taken each season from this 15-mile long spate river; and future prospects are bright, since all netting in Melvich Bay has recently been ended.

Summer fishing can be difficult due to lack of water; sometimes it is possible to cross the river almost dry-shod, but attempts have been made to create compensation flow by damming the principal feeder streams.

Best sport is on the Lower River, with good sea-trout fishing in the slow-moving waters of the estuary; Upper Halladale, from Trantlemore, is more Highland in character, rushing through steep-sided gorges, over tumbled rocks, and through peat-stained pools. Forsinard Hotel manages the Upper Halladale fishing, and the heaviest salmon taken was a splendid fish weighing 30 lb 8 oz.

Ownership of the Halladale changed in 1989, and future access to fishing is uncertain. The previous owners sold some fishing to timeshare and the remainder has been purchased by Mr J Bulmer. Forsinard Hotel is also being re-let; therefore, check before booking. But do book, because Halladale, given good water levels, is one of the most delightful salmon streams in Scotland's far north.

The Naver and Loch Naver

LOCATION: Ordnance Survey Second Series, 1:50,000. Sheets 10, Strathnaver, and 16, Lairg and Loch Shin.

GRID REFERENCES: Sheet 10 Bettyhill, 707618; Syre, 694439; **Sheet 16** Mallart, 676375; Loch Choire, 635285; Loch Naver, 620370; Altnaharra, 570352.

SEASON: February 10–September 30.

FLIES: Green Highlander, Shrimp Fly, General Practitioner, Munro Killer, Garry Dog, Willie Gunn, Hairy Mary.

COSTS: Anticipate £2,000 per week per beat on the River Naver. Loch Naver is fished from the Altnaharra Hotel and costs in the order of £50 per day, for two rods, including boat, outboard engine, fuel and gillie.

PERMISSION: River Naver; Naver and District Fishery Board, Dalvina, Strathnaver, Kinbrace, Sutherland (Tel: 06416–200). Loch Naver: Altnaharra Hotel, Altnaharra, by Lairg, Sutherland (Tel: 054981-222).

THE NAVER AND Loch Naver lie to the west of Strath Halladale. The river is a closely guarded preserve and permission to fish is almost impossible to obtain. A pre-requisite is to be on the list of one of the owners, and even then, prospective anglers may wait years before being given an opportunity to fish this famous stream.

Loch Naver is much more readily available to visiting anglers and can produce spectacular sport. This six-mile long loch fishes best during the early season, from February onwards, and although it is often cold, hard work, fighting sea-liced salmon, fresh from the Atlantic, more than make up for frozen fingers.

Autumn sport can also be good on Loch Naver, with the added bonus of excellent runs of sea-trout to brighten days when salmon are dour. The average weight of salmon is in the order of 8 lb, while sea-trout average around 1 lb 12 oz. Loch Naver also holds good stocks of wild brown trout, averaging 8 oz; but most seasons produce trout, of more than 4 lb. Be prepared!

LIVING HISTORY

The Naver, arguably the best far north-of-Scotland salmon stream, has a 10-year average of 455 fish caught. It flows out of Loch Naver, collecting in the cold waters of the Mallart, and runs 22 miles to the sea in Torrisdale Bay, by Bettyhill. Its banks are kissed purple with heather and graced by slender silver birch, and Strath Naver is a constant delight, a living museum of Highland history, where people have lived and worked since Mesolithic times.

Bettyhill, named after Elizabeth, Countess Duchess of Sutherland, stands at the mouth of the river; and it was to this rocky eminence that 2,000 crofters in the strath were ruthlessly evicted early in the nineteenth century. The Duchess and her husband, the Marquess of Stafford, reputed to be the richest man in Europe, hoped to generate more income from letting their land to sheep-farmers than from the £15,000 annual rent produced by their crofter tenants. Stafford sometimes spent that amount in a day, shopping for antiques at Christie's in London.

UNATTAINABLE DREAMS

The year of the first clearances, 1814, became known as *Bliadhna an Losgaidh*, the Year of the Burning; and when the Marquess eventually died, his wife ordered a monument to be erected on Eldrable Hill, overlooking the east-coast village of Golspie and his vast home, Dunrobin Castle. But when the statue was unveiled, the Duchess was dismayed to find that the figure of her husband had been placed looking out to sea, rather than inland, across his northern domains. She was told by her few remaining tenants that since it was to sea that Stafford had sent most of his people, to exile overseas, then it was to sea that he should be looking.

The Naver has 50 named pools divided among its six beats. The flow of water downstream is reasonably maintained by controlling levels in Loch Choire, on the north side of Ben Klibreck.

These dark, peat-stained waters quickly turn Naver into a raging, brown torrent after rains; but the river soon settles, allowing fishing to continue after a few days.

Naver salmon average about 9 lb, and since the river presents no major obstacles to returning fish, fresh salmon can be caught throughout the system from opening day onwards. The river has it own salmon hatchery, and each year eggs are stripped, hatched, and the fry planted out in headwater feeder streams.

The Naver owners operate a unique system. Each beat is restricted to two rods, and they must be a man and a boy or a woman; the belief seems to be that the boy, or woman, will not catch as many salmon as the man, which is something not always borne out in fact!

In 1988, the Syre Beat of the Naver was sold for an estimated price of £3 m. The sale included rights to two rods on Naver, fishing on Loch Naver, thousands of acres of moorlands, and several fine brown trout lochs. Syre sold quickly. Owning a beat on the Naver is every salmon angler's dream, although few can afford to.

The Borgie

LOCATION: Ordnance Survey Second Series, 1:50,000. Sheet 10, Strathnaver.

GRID REFERENCES: Torrisdale Bay, 682612; Borgie Bridge, 669588; Falls Pool, 641547.

SEASON: February 10–September 30.

FLIES: Black Doctor, Willie Gunn, Garry Dog, Shrimp Fly, Waddingtons.

COSTS: One week with comfortable, self-catering accommodation varies from £620 in early spring to £700 in May; fishing alone costs from £250/£350 per beat per week for two rods.

PERMISSION: Contact Jamie & Partners, Rectory Place, Loughborough, Leicestershire, LE11 1UR (Tel: 0509–23343).

THE A836 ROAD along Scotland's north coast climbs from Strathnaver over Druim Chuibhe, past the Stone Age hut circles at Invernaver, then down to the glen of the Borgie River and its seven miles of 'dream fishing'. It is an excellent spate river, with good runs of both salmon and sea-trout and in a fabulous setting. The best time to 'attack' the Borgie is in May, when the salmon are in splendid condition. Four rotating beats, allow anglers to fish the whole river during the course of a week.

RIVER BORGIE. The famous Falls Pool where most salmon are taken each year. For these unlucky anglers it is a prime spot to watch their elusive quarry battle their way upstream and out of 'rods way'.

The Borgie has been much improved over the years, by the creation of weirs, casting positions, pools and runs. The only major obstacle to returning fishing is the high falls, between Beats 3 and 4; but Falls Pool is one of the most productive, and certainly one of the most lovely, salmon pools in the north.

The Borgie begins life in little Loch Coulside, south from windy Loch Loyal, flowing through Lochs Loyal, Craggie and Slaim on its short, turbulent journey to the sea amid the shining sands of Torrisdale Bay. Its estuary is where most sea-trout are caught, before the Borgie Bridge. This is day-ticket water, and, given good water levels, sport can be fast and furious.

About 300 salmon are taken from the Borgie in most seasons for an average weight of around 6 lb, although fish 10 lb and more are often caught. Increasing numbers of salmon are being taken in the headwater lochs, Slaim and Craggie; and although a few undoubtedly travel on into Loch Loyal, they are rarely seen or caught in this deep, four-and-a-half-mile long water.

A week's salmon fishing on the Borgie may not send you home with many fish, but it will leave you with enchanting memories of a delightful holiday by a beautiful, fast-flowing stream.

Loch Hope

LOCATION: Ordnance Survey Second Series, 1:50,000. Sheet 9, Cape Wrath.

GRID REFERENCES: North End boats, 474599; Middle Bay boats, 467543; South End boats, 462532.

SEASON: Salmon June 12–September 30.

FLIES: Black Pennell, Ke-He, Loch Ordie, Soldier Palmer, Invicta, Grouse and Claret, Greenwell's Glory, Woodcock and Hare-lug, Butcher, Alexandra, Peter Ross.

COSTS: North End, per week, with boat, outboard motor, fuel, two rods fishing, £166.75; daily rate, £28.75. South End and Middle Bay, per week, with boat, outboard (where allowed), gillie and two rods fishing, £60.

PERMISSION: North End – Mrs P S Murch, Osberton Grange Farms, Scofton, Worksop, Nottinghamshire S81 0UF (Tel: 0909–472651/485621); South End – Altnaharra Hotel, Altnaharra, by Lairg, Sutherland (Tel: 095481–222).

OVER THE HILL from the Borgie lies one of the most beautiful lochs in all Scotland, Loch Hope; six miles of sheer delight and probably the far north's premier sea-trout fishery. Hope is divided into five beats: North End, Middle Bay and South End, with the last made up of Beats 1/2/3.

South End – that is, the 'upstream' end – produces best sport, although this may well be because it is more frequently fished. Recently,

North End, close to the sea, has begun to give better results as more anglers discover the delights of Loch Hope. Now, returns seem to be improving every year.

Loch Hope fishes best in July and August, although in 1989 the first sea-trout, a fine fish weighing 7 lb, was taken on an Alexandra Streamer from South End, where the waters of the Strathmore river enter the loch, on June 22.

Brown trout of considerable size are also encountered in Loch Hope: in 1987 Mr Nicoll had a fish of 6 lb to a Black Pennell, and later that year two further 'monster' brown trout were landed, one of 7 lb 13 oz and one of 7 lb taken from Beats 1 and 3 by Mr Gamble and Mr R Mackenzie.

Outboard motors are not allowed, on some beats of South End for fear of disturbing the sea-trout in the shallow water close to where the Strathmore River comes in, and fishing is therefore not always possible when high winds are blowing. Indeed, even in normal conditions, unless you have a gillie, be prepared for some hard rowing – or pack a strong young friend to wield the oars while you fish.

Dapping is a favourite and much-used technique on Hope. The dap is used to tempt a fish to rise, and then lifted from the water at the last moment and, hopefully, the sea-trout turns right or left to grab the traditional wet flies being fished by the rod at bow or stern. Being in the right place at the right time is all-important; and having the services of an experienced gillie greatly improves an angler's chance of success on Hope.

Salmon also run into the loch and are sometimes caught – about a dozen fish each season – but sea-strout are the principal quarry, and draw anglers from all over the world.

LOCH HOPE. The quiet before the storm. Her waters offer anglers six miles of first class sea-trout fishing amongst some of northern Scotland's finest scenery. Both brown trout and sea-trout of 7 lb have been caught.

Cape Wrath

LOCATION: Ordnance Survey Second Series, 1:50,000. Sheet 9, Cape Wrath.

GRID REFERENCES: Cape Wrath Hotel, 380663; River Dionard, 360610; Loch Dionard, 356490; Loch Caladail, 397667; Loch Lanlish, 385684; Loch Borralie, 384670; Loch Croispol, 390680.

SEASON: Salmon – February 10–September 30. Trout – April 1–September 30.

FLIES: Salmon – Silver Wilkinson, Hairy Mary, Garry Dog, Shrimp Fly, General Practitioner, Munro Killer, Goat's Toe, Waddingtons. Sea-trout – Black Pennell, Ke-He, Invicta, Soldier Palmer, Grouse and Green, Teal, Blue and Silver, Peter Ross. Brown trout – Greenwell's Glory, March Brown, Black Pennell, Invicta, Soldier Palmer, Grouse and Claret, Dunkeld, Black Zulu, Blue Zulu, Butcher.

COSTS: Salmon and sea-trout fishing is approximately £18 per rod per day. To fish the brown trout loch is £18 per day for a boat for two rods.

PERMISSION: Cape Wrath Hotel, Keodale, Durness, by Lairg, Sutherland (Tel: 097182–274).

STRATH DIONARD AND Cape Wrath, to the west of Loch Hope, is an angler's dream come true. The area has something for everyone: sparkling salmon and sea-trout from the River Dionard; outstanding wild brown trout of the highest quality from the famous Durness limestone lochs; and the exciting, remote lochs of The Parph (Cape Wrath), where baskets of 20 or more breakfast-sized trout are the rule rather than the exception.

The Dionard rises amid the wild corries and glens of Foinaven and Creagan Meall Horn, flowing 12 miles north from its loch through the magnificent, silent land of Strath Dionard to greet the sea among the sands of the Kyle of Durness.

This is greenshank country, where the plaintiff, incessant piping of these lovely birds accompanies your casting. The mountains are scattered with lichen-covered boulders, and bog myrtle, heather and cloudberry scent the summer air. It is one of Scotland's special places.

Salmon run the Dionard from February onwards, but the best sport is from June to September, with sea-trout at their peak in July. Most salmon are taken in the lower river, the upper reaches being fast-flowing and rocky, with few good holding pools.

When conditions on the river are difficult, Loch Dionard can provide spectacular sport; it has a comfortable fishing hut where guests may spend a few nights, to avoid wasting good fishing time in making the long trek back to civilisation.

The average weight of Dionard salmon is a modest 7 lb and the river produces about 100 fish each season; but good numbers of heavier fish are caught, with fish of more than 20 lb landed on occasion. Sea-trout of more than 5 lb are also taken although the average is around 1½ lb.

If both river and loch are out of sorts, then most anglers head for the limestone trout lochs: Caladail, Borralie, Lanlish and Croispol. They contain wild brown trout of the highest quality; perfectly-shaped, pink-fleshed and fighting-fit.

EXPERT FISHING

Lanlish, smallest of the Durness lochs, produces the largest fish, with trout of more than 10 lb taken in times past. Even today, Lanlish produces fish of more than 8 lb. Caladail trout are not so large, but golden-coloured; a recent basket from this superb loch was four fish together weighing 15 lb.

Borralie, the deepest of these spring-fed limestone lochs, also holds wonderful brown trout and stocks of Arctic char. Croispol fish are just as spectacular, but more numerous and small, although a few years ago Professor Norman Simmonds, from Edinburgh, surprised everyone, including himself, by landing a Croispol trout which weighed 4 lb 8 oz.

The Durness limestone lochs are not for beginners; blank days are frequent, even among the 'experts'. Their waters are crystal-clear, and the slightest casting misdemeanour sends trout scurrying to safety. But to visit Cape Wrath and not fish these amazing lochs would be an unforgivable angling sin. They are, quite simply, outstanding.

Scourie and Loch Stack

LOCATION: Ordnance Survey Second Series, 1:50,000. Sheet 9, Cape Wrath; Sheet 15, Loch Assyut.

GRID REFERENCES: Sheet 9, Scourie Hotel, 156450; **Sheet 15**, Reay Forest Estate Office, 292396; West End boats, 271437; East End boats, 299413.

SEASON: February 10–September 30

FLIES: Loch Ordie, Ke-He, Invicta, Bibio, Soldier Palmer, Black Zulu, Teal, Blue and Silver, Black Pennell, Grouse and Claret, Alexandra, Dunkeld, Kingfisher Butcher, Peter Ross.

COSTS: Reay Forest Estate and Scourie Hotel: £35 per boat per day for two rods.

PERMISSION: Reay Forest Estate, Lochmore, Achfary, by Lairg, Sutherland, IV27 4PQ (Tel: 097184–221). Reay Forest Estate has comfortably-furnished self-catering cottages to let with fishing on Lochs Stack and More. Scourie Hotel, Scourie, by Lairg, Sutherland (Tel: 0971–2396). Scourie Hotel offers all-inclusive gamefishing holidays on its brown-trout lochs; and salmon and sea-trout fishing on Lochs Stack and More, when available, and on other salmon and sea-trout systems in the vicinity.

SOUTHWARDS FROM STRATH Dionard, the A838 climbs to the watershed at Gualin House, then drops swiftly into the valley of the Laxford River, an excellent, but completely private salmon stream owned by the Duke of Westminster. Anglers stop on Laxford Bridge to ponder over the unattainable, but not for long, because attainable angling dreams abound at nearby Scourie, a first-class fishing centre, famed for the number and quality of its wild brown-trout lochs. Scourie Hotel offers fishing on more than 300 waters. The best of them involves a long walk, but it's worth every step of the way.

But the principal fishing water in the area is glorious Loch Stack, easily accessible and generally available either through the Reay Forest Estate of Scourie Hotel. Stack is among Scotland's best-loved and most productive sea-trout waters. It also produces good numbers of salmon and excellent sport with brown trout.

HARD-EARNED REWARDS

But best things of life rarely come easy, and Stack is no exception. A strict rule prohibits the use of outboard motors, and gillies are not readily available. So, be prepared for some hard work on the oars because Stack can be fierce, wild and windy.

Stack is a delightful loch to fish, full of corners and bays where sea-trout and salmon lie. Indeed most fish are taken close to the shores, away from deep water; and North Bay, Wilson's Bay, and along the Arkle shore are among the best lies. The bays where feeder-streams enter – Uairridh Burn and the Loan Burn – are also good. Stack is joined to its less-productive neighbour, Loch More.

The time to tackle sea-trout on this system is during July and August. Advance booking is essential. Stack fishing is much sought-after.

The Inver, Kirkaig and Loch Assynt

LOCATION: Ordnance Survey Second Series, 1:50,000. Sheet 15, Assynt and Lochinver.

GRID REFERENCES: Lochinver, 095225; Loch Assynt, 200250; Inchnadamph, 250221; Kirkaig Bridge, 085193; Kirkaig Falls, 113177.

SEASON: February 10–September 30.

FLIES: Thunder and Lightning, Garry Dog, Green Highlander, Black Doctor, Munro Killer, General Practitioner, Shrimp Fly, Waddingtons, Mar Lodge.

COSTS: For Inver and Kirkaig, about £30 per rod per day; Loch Assynt, with boat for two rods, £15 per day.

PERMISSION: Inver Lodge Hotel, Lochinver, Sutherland (Tel: 05714–496); Inchnadamph Hotel, Inchnadamph, Assynt, Sutherland (Tel: 05712–202).

LOCHINVER, ASSYNT AND Inchnadamph, south from Scourie, offer a wide range of gamefishing. The Assynt Angling Club has trout-fishing on more than 30 productive lochs between Lochinver and Assynt, including useful sea-trout fishing on Loch Roag; but the prime waters are the rivers Inver and Kirkaig, and Loch Assynt, controlled by local hotels, all of which can provide excellent salmon-fishing from June onwards.

The Inver is a wide, slow-moving stream,

RIVER INVER. The largest fish, 27 lb 4 oz, taken from here was a ferox trout, in 1870, by Dr H Almond. For those in search of summer salmon this remote river offers first class sport. The best fly to try is a Thunder and Lightning.

flowing six miles from Loch Assynt to the sea in Inver Bay. Because of a dam at the West end of Assynt, the Inver maintains reasonable water levels throughout the season. It is divided into two beats, Upper and Lower.

Fishing on Lower Inver is rarely available to casual visitors, but the most productive time to fish is from June to August. Salmon average 8 lb, although fish of 16 lb or more are caught most years.

Upper Inver produces about 40 salmon each season, but in a good year more than 100 may be caught: 1988 produced 98 fish. The upper river has a series of fine pools, including Black Pool, which in 1989 gave one fortunate angler three fish for 22 lb, all taken on a size 8 Thunder and Lightning. Gravestones, Mill, Carpenter's and Upper Rocky Pool all have their moments; and Weir Pool, on Lower Inver, is the place to hunt for sea-trout, particularly during June and July.

DEGREES OF DIFFICULTY

Unsually, the largest fish taken from the Inver was a brown trout, not a salmon. It was reputed to weigh 27 lb 4 oz, and no doubt was a wandering *ferox* from Loch Assynt. It was caught by Dr H H Almond in 1870.

The Kirkaig lies along the boundary between Sutherland and Ross-shire; four miles of turbulent, dashing stream, carving a hard granite path from the Fionn Loch to the sea in Kirkaig Bay.

Below the road-bridge and county boundary, the Kirkaig pauses, as though to catch its breath after its head-long journey down from Suilven, Scotland's most photographed mountain, known to the Vikings as Sul-val, the Pillar Mountain.

Then, the rivers last few hundred yards are slow and deep, enclosing wide pools where salmon rest as they come in from the cold Atlantic tides.

Kirkaig is divided into three beats: Upper, Middle and Lower: They almost prescribe the sort of angler most suited to tackling them: Upper, for fit, athletic youngsters; Middle, for those who still think they are fit, athletic youngsters; Lower, for anglers prepared to face the sad facts of advancing years and diminishing breath.

However, every beat has its own special character and challenge – from the Falls Pool at the head of the river, where anglers risk life and limb to scramble down to the fishing stance, to the utterly beautiful, deep, dark pools of Middle River.

About 100 salmon and 50 sea-trout are taken off the Kirkaig each season, the salmon averaging 9 lb 8 oz, the sea-trout 1 lb 8 oz. July is usually the best month, and in 1988 that month produced the bulk of the annual catch, with 52 salmon and grilse caught. The heaviest fish taken in 1989 was a fine salmon of 16 lb. It was landed by Mr N C Glazebrook from Elder Pool on the Lower River.

If the water level is unkind, or the weather too bright, too wet, or too windy, or if things are just downright miserable, the Kirkaig offers the next best thing to fishing: reading about fishing. Close to the car-park at Kirkaig Bridge is the remotest bookshop on mainland Scotland: Achairn's well stocked with angling books designed to cheer even the dullest spirit.

LOCH ASSYNT. Joined to the sea by the River Inver. Climbing skywards around her shores are Ben More Assynt, (998 m) Quinag (809 m) and to the south grow the shadowy slopes of Canisp (847 m).

Loch Assynt, at the top of the Inver, is home to huge ferox trout, thousands of small, wild brown trout, and good numbers of salmon and grilse, all ready and waiting to give themselves up to a carefully-presented fly.

A less-willing resident of Assynt was the unfortunate Duke of Montrose, imprisoned at Ardvreck Castle on the eastern shore in 1650. Montrose, an ardent royalist, landed in Orkney early that year in an attempt to restore Charles II to the throne of England. Then, after being defeated in battle near the Kyle of Sutherland, he fled westwards into the wild lands of the Macleods of Assynt.

HIGHLAND HOSPITALITY

The clan chief offered him shelter in Ardvreck, but as soon as Montrose was secured, Macleod turned traitor, locked the Duke in a dungeon and betrayed him to the authorities in Edinburgh. He was taken to Edinburgh, tied to the back of a Highland pony, tried and beheaded. His body was dismembered and parts were distributed throughout the Highlands to discourage further attempts at rebellion.

One of King Charles II's first acts in 1660 was to gather in poor Montrose's remains; they were honourably interred in St Giles Cathedral. As for the Macleods of Assynt, from the day they betrayed the principal of Highland hospitality, their fortunes declined and their race withered.

But Highland hospitality can be found today in Assynt at Inchnadamph Hotel, presided over by Willie Morrison, who will point visitors in the right direction for Loch Assynt salmon and wish them 'Tight lines' in their efforts.

The Oykel

LOCATION: Ordnance Survey Land Ranger Series, 1:50,000. **Sheets 15**, Loch Assynt and 16, Lairg and Loch Shin.

GRID REFERENCES: Sheet 15 Ailsh, 315105; **Sheet 16 Rosehall, 477015.**

SEASON: January 11–September 30.

FLIES: Hairy Mary, Willie Gunn, Garry Dog, Munro Killer, Shrimp Fly, General Practitioner, Black Doctor, Goat's Toe, Waddingtons.

COSTS: About £35 per rod per day.

PERMISSION: Lower Oykel – Finlayson Hughes, Estate Office, Bonar Bridge, Sutherland (Tel: 08632–553). Upper Oykel – Oykel Bridge Hotel, Rosehall, by Lairg, Sutherland (Tel: 059984–218). Loch Ailish – Inver Lodge Hotel, Lochinver, Sutherland (Tel: 05714–496).

THE OYKEL, ONE of Sutherland's most prolific salmon streams, is born amid the high corries of mighty Ben More Assynt. It hurries south through Loch Ailsh, then eastwards, down Strath Oykel, a classic Highland glen, rowan-banked, flanked on either side by heather-clad slopes.

Oykel salmon-fishing is prized and always in demand; and anglers should book early, at least a year in advance, to have any chance of securing a rod.

The river is divided into two sections: Upper Oykel, from Loch Ailsh down to Oykel Falls; and Lower Oykel, from Oykel Falls to the meeting with the Cassley. From there, the Oykel meanders gently into the Kyle of Sutherland, mingling with its neighbours, Shin and Carron.

Glen Oykel has been much afforested in recent years, and this has lead to a shifting of traditional spawning beds; although the Kyle of Sutherland Fishery Board has done a considerable amount of work to improve the river by constructing groynes to control the flow.

From its source to the Kyle, Oykel changes in character from tumbling rapids to gentle pools, crystal-clear under the summer sun, when most salmon run the river. Upwards of 1,500 salmon are taken most seasons, Lower Oykel producing best sport during the early months, and Upper Oykel coming into its own after spring spates encourage salmon upstream.

Noted pools on the lower river are George, Blue, Langwell, Junction, and (Einag) Falls. The upper river begins to fish from late May, although the best sport is not until July. From then until September, the upper river can provide superb results with salmon which average 9 lb and grilse averaging 5 lb.

It is also an outstandingly beautiful river to fish. At Oykel Falls, white waters thunder over time-worn, steel-grey limestone rocks; the scent of Scots pine and yellow gorse mingle in the breeze; hills are blazed purple with heather during autumn; and salmon fishing is at its finest. And just how good that can be is shown by the results over the last four years . . .

Oykel fishing returns 1986–1989			
OYKEL	UPPER	LOWER	LOCH AILSH
1986	216	1,153	90
1987	242	952	93
1988	329	2,043	131
1989	T/C	623 (until July 31)	

RIVER OYKEL. Long awaited autumn rains begin to fall at Bridge of Oykel. Summer of 1989 has seen these seething rapids drain to a mere trickle. On Lower Oykel over two thousand fish were taken in 1988.

The Cassley

LOCATION: Ordnance Survey Sheet 16, Lairg and Loch Shin. (Second Series, 1:50,000).

GRID REFERENCES: Hotel, 473024; Glencassley Castle, 441077; Glenmuick, 396128.

SEASON: February 22–September 30.

FLIES: Munro Killer, Blue Charm, Tadpole, Willie Gunn, Collie Dog, General Practitioner, Stoat's Tail.

COST: Prices range from £100 per week for a two-rod beat on Glenrossal in June and July to £500 per week for a three-rod beat on Lower Cassley during September.

PERMISSION: N W Graesser, MIFM, Fishery Consultant, Rosehall, by Lairg, Sutherland (Tel: 054984–202). Achness House Hotel, Rosehall, by Lairg, Sutherland (Tel: 054984–239). Upper Cassley Fishing – Bell Ingram, Estate Agents, Bonar Bridge, Sutherland (Tel: 08632–632).

RIVER CASSLEY. A beautiful Highland spate river. The thundering waters race to meet with the Oykel. The swirling pools and tumbling rapids shelter salmon of up to 20 lb, perhaps one with your name on it.

THE CASSLEY, THE principal tributary of the Oykel, is a delightful Highland spate stream that provides excellent salmon fishing, given good water levels. It is a rocky, urgent stream, with attractive pools and fast, turbulent runs: Craig, Road Pool, Lower Platform, Round Pool and Cemetery Pool are a few of the most notable.

The river has prolific runs of grilse during June, and salmon of up to 20 lb are sometimes taken. The water is easily accessible and can be fished comfortably from the bank without much need for wading, though some agility is needed to cover some of the lies – and a fair degree of accuracy in casting. But this is all part of the pleasure of fishing the Cassley, where something new and challenging is around every bend of the river.

Cassley is divided into three beats: Beat 1, from the Falls, downstream to the Bridge; Beat 2, from Falls upstream to the Boundary, and from the Bridge to the tail of Lower Dyke; and Beat 3, from the Barrier Pool to the mouth of the river in the Kyle of Sutherland.

A condition of letting is that anglers stay at the Achness House Hotel, Rosehall, a comfortable fishing hotel which has been extended recently by the building of a new wing.

Around 300 salmon and grilse are taken most seasons and, as on the Oykel fishing is always in demand. Book early and pray for rain.

The Shin and Loch Craggie

LOCATION: Ordnance Survey Second Series, 1:50,000. Sheets 16, Lairg and Loch Shin, and 21, Dornoch Firth.

GRID REFERENCES: Sheet 21 Lairg, 575666; Shin Falls, 576994; **Sheet 16** Loch Craggie, 625075.

SEASON: Shin (salmon), January 11–September 30; Loch Craggie (trout), April 1–September 30.

FLIES: Shin – Hairy Mary, Collie Dog, General Practitioner, Willie Gunn, Silver Wilkinson, Munro Killer, Waddingtons. Loch Craggie – Ke-He, Black Pennell, Invicta, Soldier Palmer, Greenwell's Glory, March Brown, Black Zulu, Blue Zulu, Butcher, Dunkeld, Peter Ross.

COST: Shin (salmon), £25 per rod per day; Loch Craggie (trout), £30 per day per boat for two rods.

PERMISSION: Sutherland Arms Hotel, Lairg, Sutherland (Tel: 0549–2291).

RIVER SHIN. Magnificent Falls of Shin is the place to watch salmon leaping. Again and again a fish will battle to jump these falls. A fight with a salmon, successful or not will remain with the angler as one of the highlights of his career.

THE KYLE OF Sutherland rivers, Shin, Oykel, Cassley and Carron, have been much affected in recent years by hydro-electric dams. The glory days of Kyle salmon fishing have long since gone, and anglers who fished these rivers before the headwaters were impounded shake their heads sadly. Nevertheless, salmon still run the rivers in considerable numbers, and the Shin, although but a shadow of its former self, is still one of the north's best salmon streams.

Water-flow down the Shin is controlled by the ugly, high dam across the east end of Loch Shin; the grey structure dominates this small Sutherland town and concern has been expressed by local people over the consequences to their community should torrential rain ever breach the dam. The Falls of Shin form the major natural obstacle to returning salmon. White water thunders over the falls at times of heavy rain; and visitors come from far and wide to watch salmon leaping the foaming torrent.

Paradise Pool, famous for huge fish, was washed away in floods in 1988; but the riparian owners quickly repaired the damage. The Shin is a well managed, delightful river, well worth a cast or two or three or more. More than 400 salmon are taken in most seasons.

For those who prefer brown-trout fishing, or for salmon angler's when 'fish' are dour and hard to tempt, Loch Craggie, to the north of Lairg, is one of the finest waters in Scotland. Fish average about 12 oz, but much heavier trout are there and specimen fish of the highest quality are frequently taken. Craggie offers splendid sport in splendid surroundings, and rarely sends anglers home empty-handed.

The Brora and Helmsdale

LOCATION: Ordnance Survey Second Series 1:50,000. Sheet 17, Strath of Kildonan.

GRID REFERENCES: Brora, 905040; Loch Brora, 850080; Balnacoil, 810112; Helmsdale, 027155.

SEASON: Brora – February 1–October 15; Helmsdale – January 11–September 30.

FLIES: Green Highlander, Hairy Mary, Shrimp Fly, Willie Gunn, Garry Dog, Pilkington, Stoat's Tail, and Bill Currie's Black and Yellow and Black and Orange Brora Waddington's.

COSTS: On the Brora, anticipate up to £2,000 per week for a lodge sleeping 14–16 people, with four rods on the river. Loch Brora costs about £25 per day for a boat for two rods. Salmon and sea-trout fishing is sometimes available on Brora Town Water at a cost of £10 per rod per day. On the Helmsdale; the association water costs about £18 per rod per day.

PERMISSION: Brora and Loch Brora: Colin Taylor, Rob Wilson (Guns and Tackle), Brora, Sutherland (Tel: 0408–21373). The Factor, The Sutherland Estate, Duke Street, Golspie, Sutherland (Tel: Golspie 04083–3268). The Royal Marine Hotel Brora (Tel: 0408–21251) offers inclusive gamefishing holidays on Loch Brora.

NORTH FROM THE Kyle of Sutherland, and flowing into the cold waters of the North Sea, are two of Scotland's most outstanding salmon rivers, the Brora and the Helmsdale.

The Brora rises close to the source of the Naver, flowing from the slopes of Creag Riabhach na Greighe as a tumbling Highland stream and passes swiftly through a vast, wild land to the weir at Dalnessie.

Victorian shooting-lodges grace the banks of the Brora as the river hurries past Grumby Rock to civilisation at Dalrevoch, swinging in a wide arc, north and east, to collect in the waters of its main tributary, the Blackwater, at Balnacoil Lodge.

From there, Brora slows into a tangle of ox-bow bends, before emptying into Loch Brora, a series of three interlinked basins. Three-and-a-half miles further east, the river bustles through the little town of Brora into the sea.

SWIFT SWIMMING SALMON

The river is divided into three: Lower River, from the sea to Loch Brora; Loch Brora; and Upper River, including the Blackwater. Rods are difficult to obtain on Lower River and almost impossible to book on Upper River, where most of the fishing is let in conjunction with estate lodges, which carry shooting as well as fishing rights.

Salmon tend to run quickly upstream during the early months of the season, through the loch and into the Upper River; consequently, rods are sometimes available on the Lower River during spring, and good catches can be taken. But the best of the sport on Brora is on the Upper River and Blackwater. Year after year, the same people return to Sutherland Estate Lodges, but it is always worth inquiring to see if there has been a cancellation.

The most readily available fishing is on Loch Brora, although even that should be booked well in advance. Here the best sport is with sea-trout. Large numbers of these sporting fish run the Brora from June onwards, and most are taken in the loch. Fly-only is the rule, and sea-trout of more than 6 lb have been landed.

NATIVE KNOW-HOW

Each of the three sections of the loch can produce sport, but an angler with limited time would do well to seek local advice. The place to find it is at Rob Wilson's tackle-shop in Brora, a Mecca for generations of anglers. Colin Taylor now owns the business, although Rob Wilson can often be found there, offering advice with his customary charm and kindness.

If the opportunity arises to fish in company with a local angler, it should not be missed. It could mean the difference between an empty basket and a red-letter day. Say 'Yes', instantly!

Many notable salmon have been landed from the Brora, but perhaps one of the best was caught by Rob Wilson's brother, John. It weighed 40 lb and was caught in the Bengie Pool in 1958.

Even more remarkable than the size of the fish was the means of its capture. Rob had just built a new $2\frac{3}{4}$ oz trout rod and had asked his brother to try it on the river. John saw the big fish move and eventually took it on a size 8 Green Highlander. It

was landed after a great fight of one-and-a-half hours.

The Town Water apart, if you had an arm and a leg to spare, it would not be enough to get a day's fishing on the Helmsdale, one of the most exclusive salmon rivers in Europe. In August, 1989, Helmsdale's six beats averaged 10 salmon and grilse per day, each, and the system generally produces up to 3,000 fish every season. Salmon average around 9 lb, and sea-trout, of which good numbers run the river, average 2 lb.

For most anglers, then, the Town Water offers the only opportunity to fish this first-class river; and although you may be told that most salmon run straight through the lower water, this beat does produce upwards of 250 salmon each season, a figure that would put many popular beats to shame.

As always, advance booking is essential, as is being in the right place at the right time. Fish are taken throughout the season on the Town Water, but autumn probably offers the best opportunity for success.

RIVER BRORA. The Lower Brora Beat can sometimes give anglers first class sport in spring and although not as good as upper reaches it is much easier to get a day on. Sea-trout fishing along here and on Loch Brora is also superb.

3. The Spey

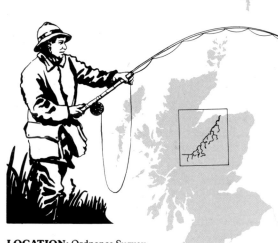

LOCATION: Ordnance Survey
Land Ranger Series, 1:50,000. Sheets
34, Fort Augustus; 35, Kingussie; 36,
Grantown and Cairngorm; and 28, Elgin.

GRID REFERENCES: Sheet 34, Loch Spey, 420937.
Sheet 35, Spey Dam, 582935; Loch Inch, 830045. **Sheet 36,**
Boat of Barten, 947192; Spey Bridge, 040264; Craigory,
055273; Cromdale, 066288; Dalriach, 087317. **Sheet 28,**
Tulchan, 132356; Avon Junction Pool, 175370; Pitchory,
178380; Aberlour, 265426; Craigellachie Bridge, 285453;
Arndilly House, 291472; Rothes, 278495; Delfur, 318523.

SEASONS: Salmon – February 11–September 30. Best time
for salmon is late spring and early summer. Good sport can be
had sometimes in autumn, but fish are often coloured. Trout –
March 15–September 30. Best months, late May, June July.

FLIES: Salmon – Munro Killer, Stoat's Tail, Lady Caroline,
Stuart's Killer, Silver Doctor, Jeannie, Arndilly Fancy, Delfur
Fancy. Trout – Peter Ross, Stuart's Special, Grouse and
Claret, Silver Sedge.

COSTS: The upper reaches of Spey are excellent value for
money. Badenoch Angling Association has 15 miles of the
upper river and surrounding lochs, with membership costing
£15 per year. Expect to pay £2.50 for a day or about £10 for a
week on these waters.

Down at Boat of Garten, expect to pay £28 for a week's
salmon and trout fishing. To fish around Grantown-on-Spey
will cost £30 per rod a week. But world-famous Tulchan beats
on middle Spey will cost £911 per week per rod during the
prime fishing months of May, June and July and from August
28 until September 23. First-class accommodation at Tulchan
Lodge will cost an additional £105–£155 a night.

Most middle-Spey fishings are timeshared or private.
Access is by dreams only. But wherever you go in Spey,
remember to book your fishing well in advance. Spey,
especially around Grantown, can become quite a crowded
river, its banks as full of people as its waters are of salmon and
sea-trout.

The Craigellachie fishing will cost £75 a week or £13 a day
at prime times.

The local tourist offices will provide plenty of suggestions
for non-fishing members of a party – following the whisky
trail, perhaps . . . ? Useful addresses are:

Aviemore and Spey Valley Tourist Organisation,
Grampian Road,   Aviemore, Inverness-shire (Tel: 0479–
810545).

Banff and Buchan Tourist Board, Collie Lodge, Banffshire
(Tel: 02612–2789).

Gordon District Tourist Board, St Nicholas House, Broad
Street, Elgin, Morayshire (Tel: 0343–2666).

PERMISSION: Upper Spey: A McDonald, 6 Gergask
Avenue, Laggan, Newtonmore, Inverness-shire.

Upper Spey: Badenoch Angling Association, Secretary, J
Dallas, Jeweller, High Street, Kingussie, Inverness-shire (Tel:
05042–229).
Upper Spey: Alvie Estate Office, Kincraig, Kingussie.
Inverness-shire (Tel: 05404–255).
Aviemore: Osprey Fishing School, Fishing Centre,
Aviemore, Inverness-shire (Tel: 0479–810767/810911).
Aviemore: Lynwilg Hotel, Loch Alvie, Aviemore, Inverness-
shire (Tel: 0479–810207).
Aviemore: Kinrara Estate Office, Aviemore, Inverness-shire
(Tel: 0479–810713).
Aviemore: Rothiemurchus Estate, Inverdrurie, Aviemore,
Inverness-shire (Tel: 0479–810858).
Boat of Garten: Craigard Hotel, Boat of Garten, Inverness-
shire (Tel: 047983–206).
Boat of Garten: Abernethy Angling Association, The Boat
Hotel, Boat of Garten, Inverness-shire (Tel: 047983–258).
Boat of Garten: Ben-o-Gar Stores, Boat of Garten,
Inverness-shire (Tel: 047983–372).
Nethybridge: Abernethy Angling Association, The Boat
Hotel, Boat of Garten, Inverness-shire (Tel: 047983–351).
Nethybridge: Tarricmor, Nethybridge, Inverness-shire (Tel:
047982–363).
Dulnain Bridge: Mrs McCafferty, Park Head Cottage, Skye
of Curr, Dulnain Bridge, Inverness-shire (Tel: 047985–219).
Grantown-on-Spey: Strathspey Angling Association,
Mortimer's, 61 High Street, Grantown-on-Spey, Morayshire
(Tel: 0479–2684).
Grantown-on-Spey: Spey Valley Hotel, Seafield Avenue,
Grantown-on-Spey, Morayshire (Tel: 0479–2942).
Grantown-on-Spey: Seafield Lodge Hotel, Grantown-on-
Spey, Morayshire (Tel: 0479–2152).
Castle Grant: Factor, Seafield Estate Office, Grantown-on-
Spey, Morayshire (Tel: 0479–2529).
Tulchan: The Factor, Tulchan, Estate Office, Alvie,
Grantown-on-Spey, Morayshire (Tel: 08075–200).
Ballindalloch Castle: Mr Russell, Estate Office,
Ballindalloch Castle, Banffshire (Tel: 08072–205).

Ballindalloch: Mr and Mrs M Blunt, Blairfindy Lodge
Hotel, Glenlivet, Ballindalloch, Banffshire (Tel: 08073–376).
Lower Wester Elchies: R and R Urquart, 121 High Street,
Forres, Morayshire (Tel: 0309–72216).
Aberlour: J Munro, 95 High Street, Aberlour, Banffshire
(Tel: 03405–220).
Aberlour: Lour Hotel, Aberlour, Banffshire (Tel:
03405–224).
Aberlour: Aberlour Hotel, Aberlour, Banffshire (Tel:
03405–287).
Aberlour: Dowans Hotel, Aberlour, Banffshire (Tel:
03405–488).
Craigellachie: Craigellachie Holdings Ltd, 55 Northgate,
Sleaford, Lincolnshire (Tel: 0529–302946).
Craigellachie: Mr W Roy, Craigmichael, Maggieknockater,
Banffshire (Tel: 03404–387).
Fochabers: Gordon Arms Hotel, Fochabers, Banffshire (Tel:
0343–820508/820509).

MAGNIFICENT SPEY, ONE of Scotland's
finest salmon rivers, is every angler's
dream. Its long course has not one obstacle to the
passage of fish, only an endless succession of long
pools and streamy rapids. Salmon can be caught
along almost the whole length of the river, still
fresh and sea-liced, from the first of the opening
spates. The prime months are May and June, but
big fish seldom move into Spey until autumn.
Spey salmon average around 11 lb, but what they
lack in size, they make up for in numbers. Spey
also offers first-class sea-trout fishing, with June
the best month for summer night fishing. The fish
average about 2½ lb.

Spey begins its 100-mile course at remote little
Loch Spey, nestling among the snow-capped

RIVER SPEY. One of
Scotlands finest
salmon and sea trout
rivers. Near Grantown,
the stillness of evening
hushes Spey's rushing
waters and silences the
wind in the pine tree's.

peaks of the Grampian Mountains. Bubbling
streams from the surrounding high, wind-swept
terrain feed the loch, and then, as soon as waters
leave the loch to form the true Spey, they are
joined by more sparkling burns gushing down the
steep slopes of Corrieyairack Forest.

Drainage from forestry plantations has led to
shorter, more dramatic and swifter spates than
formerly came down. At best, the Spey is a murky
river after rain, but when in spate its waters run
almost black.

The upper Spey is tapped for hydro-
electricity, but a mile below Spey Dam, the river
is compensated by the Mashie Burn's peaty forest
waters. From here the river meanders through
fertile pastures, guarded by purple-grey
mountains, themselves haunted by curlew and
grazed by red deer.

Among the hills lies Cluny's Cave, were Clan
Chief Cluny MacPherson hid for eight years after
the failure of the 1745 Jacobite Rebellion. He had
an excellent view from his hideout, and was able
to watch Cumberland and his Redcoats burn his
home to a pile of smouldering ashes. It was not
until the 1800s that Cluny Castle was re-built.

Downstream, Spey is joined by the Truim's
crystal waters, tumbling down Glen Truim.
Then, at Newtonmore, the Calder joins, flowing
into Glen Banchor from the rugged mountains.
Truim and the Tromie, which joins the Spey
below Kingussie, have both been 'hydroised'.

Close to the river as it flows now through a
fertile plain are the ruins of Ruthven Barracks on
their grassy mound, mute witness to one of the
few Jacobite Rebellions successes of 1745. An
attack led by Gordon of Glenbucket brought
about the fall of Government troops stationed in

RIVER SPEY. Looking upstream from Cromdale. Rain clouds roll down the valley from the Cairngorm Mountains. After such a dry summer, 1989, the rain comes as a welcome to fish and angler alike.

the garrison. Unfortunately, the Jacobite success was short-lived, for defeat at Culloden was soon to follow. So began the bloody reign of Cumberland, who ruthlessly hunted down Jacobite sympathisers throughout the Highlands.

A mile downstream from Tromie junction, Spey flows through water-logged pastures clumped with coarse rushed, sedges and bow alder until at last it spills from its course to form Loch Insh, a shallow water cradled by oak, beech, birch, willow, alder and spikes of Scots pine. For the gamefisher, the attraction of Insh is tempered by the knowledge that it holds pike, as do other sluggish reaches of upper Spey. If not controlled, these fish could decimate stocks of salmon parr, and netting keeps their number down.

A FAST RIVER

As if reluctant to leave Loch Insh, Spey swirls around a tree-clad island before bubbling on to meet its tributary Feshie, beyond Kincraig. Within this hamlet's church is the bronze Celtic hand-bell of St Eunan, carried more than 1,400 years ago at the front of funeral proccessions.

The Feshie is suffocated by forestry plantations, but it is joined by many peaty burns as it tumbles over shifting gravels, and in times of spate, these wash down black peat from the surrounding moors. Below the Feshie junction, the river takes in the Druie whose feeder burns rise close by Wells of Dee, source of another magnificent Scottish salmon river.

Snow melt from the Cairngorms ensures that the Spey is fishable for most of the season. Early spring, when the burns are still frozen, and during severe summer droughts are the only times that, normally, the river may be short of water.

By the time it reaches Aviemore, now spoiled by ugly modern buildings, Spey is justifying its reputation as a fast river. Next village down is sleepy Boat of Garten, at the foot of Abernethy Forest. Until the bridge was built here, a ferry was the means of crossing the river.

Next tributaries to join the Spey are the Nethy and Dulnain. Not far from the Nethy confluence is the tiny village of Tullochgorum, which lends its name to a famous Strathspey reel composed by Hamish Dallasach, an eighteenth-century fiddler. Dulnain, joining from the west, is an excellent salmon river in its own right.

The Spey is quite wide as it flows into Grantown-on-Spey, capital of Strathspey and seat of Clan Grant. The town dates from 1765, when Ludovic Grant proposed that it should be a centre for wool, linen and wood. Today, the town depends on tourism, but many of its visitors are also fishermen. Strathspey Angling Improvement Association has several miles of fishing open to visitors and annual returns averaging more than 300 salmon, 100 grilse, and more than 1,000 sea-trout. It is from Grantown that Arthur Oglesby runs his well-known fishing courses.

Spey salmon-fishing is at is best from Grantown down to the estuary, and as the river tumbles seawards through pastures pine, birch, hazel and beech, it seems to carry with it the misty scent of the forests left behind, a heady Highlands aroma.

Fishing these stretches of the Spey can be difficult because of the speed of the current. Wading demands the utmost care, and it's best always to have a gillie, or at least a companion, to hand. Some boat fishing is done, but usually boats are used only to ferry anglers from bank to bank.

Though they may never have fished here, most salmon anglers will know the names of the fishings – Tulcham and Castle Grant. Castle Grant No.1 Beat gave Mr D Hulme a beautiful fresh-run 31 lb salmon in 1989, and neighbouring Tulchan grossed 170 salmon in the first week of July.

Car-driving dreamers about these Spey fishings cause traffic jams along the A95, which closely follows the river's course. Fortunately, fishing isn't the only major attraction in the strath. Broken-hearted fishermen may console themselves by sampling the many local whiskys. One of the most famous is Glenlivet, named after the glen of its origin and the golden Livet burn. The Livet is, in fact not a tributary of the Spey, but of the Avon (A'an, the locals call it), joining at the foot of Hill of Deskie (408 m) and Creag an Tarmachain (646 m).

FAMOUS NAMES

The Avon's source lies high on the cold, grey granite and dazzling-white quartz slopes of the Cairngorms, and this good start in life makes it as crystal-clear as the Dee and demanding of those who come to fish it. Nevertheless, it gives up a good many salmon in a season.

The Avon meets the Spey at the famous Junction Pool at Ballindalloch, on Ballindalloch Castle Estate. The Castle, set among woodlands, dates from 1845, but has its foundations in the mid-fourteenth century. It was once the ancestral seat of Sir George MacPherson Grant. The Ballindalloch fishings are much sought-after, not least the Junction Pool. In 1987, one angler, blank with salmon, found consolation in a magnificent wild brown trout of 8 lb.

Hereabouts on Spey, famous names follow one another in quick succession: Upper Pitchroy, Lower Pitchroy, Phonas Water, Knockando, Laggan and Carron, Wester Elchies, Kinermony, Aberlour, Easter Elchies, and Craigellachie. All provide first-class sport, and all are definitely expensive.

One mile of north-bank fishing on lower Easter Elchies, opposite Craigellachie, came on to the market in late 1989 at an asking price of £900,000 for four rods fishing the six named pools. The average annual returns on the beat are 139 salmon and 50 sea-trout. 1985-87 saw more than 160 salmon taken, and 1988 and '89 accounted for 89 and 49 salmon respectively. The last figures were due to poor seasons and to the beat not being fished as hard as usual.

On Knockando tributary burn is used as a salmon hatchery run by the Spey District Salmon Board. Salmon are caught and stripped of their ova and milt, and the resultant fry are planted out over the whole Spey system.

It was hereabouts on Spey, where its steep, wooded sides make casting so difficult that the casting technique now known as Spey casting was developed. This method of switch-casting keeps the line in front of the angler at all times.

At Craigellachie the river is crossed by a beautiful single-span bridge, designed by Telford and opened in 1815. It is open now only to walkers, who come to watch sea-trout and salmon running the rapids to the Bridge Pool.

A mile downstream Spey is joined by the Fiddich, its gien home to Glenfiddich whisky and another stream born in the bleak Cairngorms, close by the source of the Livet. One reason why the Spey middle fishings are so good is that the lower waters are sometimes not cold enough to hold the salmon, and the fish move up to the middle river where the effects of the cold streams from the mountains are still felt.

But lower Spey fishings are nevertheless renowned as, from Craigellachie, Spey tumbles through the famous beats of Arndilly, Rothes, Aikenway, Delfur, Orton, Brae and magnificent Gordon Castle.

Rothes Water is overshadowed by Ben Aigan (470 m), last of the Strathspey hills. Stretching north is Speymouth Forest, a vast and ugly expanse of conifers, and then, beyond the forest, the last meandering reaches of the Spey, long, wide pools and stream around shifting islands before the river meets the sea.

YEARS OF PLENTY

Rothes Castle's decaying ruin is still to be seen. The castle was built in the early thirteenth century by the de Polloks, and it was here that hospitality and a bed were given to Edward I of England in 1296, on his return from Elgin. Edward had come north to do battle in response to the attempts by the Scottish King, Balliol, to wage war on England and join in an alliance with France. His victory over Balliol's army was helped by Scots such as Balliol's rival, Robert Bruce.

Balliol subsequently renounced his claim to the throne and was held captive for three years in the Tower of London before going to France. His place in history is not one of fame. He was known best for his weak character and as Toom Tabard, Empty Coat.

It was below Rothes on the Gordon Castle water, that Spey's largest salmon was taken in 1897. Mr W G Craven caught it in Dallachy Pool, and it tipped the scales at 53 lb. This was during the years of plenty, on Spey, when each autumn the Gordon Castle beats accounted for more than 400 salmon averaging 6–8 lb more than the fish of today.

Fish are taken from these lowest beats throughout the season. In autumn salmon of more than 20 lb are not uncommon. The Brae water yielded one fresh-run fish of 25 lb in 1989, and the same season saw a 21-pounder taken from Delfur Water. At Castle Grant fish of 28 lb 8 oz and 31 lb were caught. It's just a matter of being in the right place at the right time with the right flies – and saying the right prayers.

Spey is much wider here, and constantly eroding new courses seawards. The size of some of the pools makes boat fishing essential, but it also makes boat fishing possible as the water is slower than upstream.

The gradual buying-out of Spey nets should lead to an increase in numbers of running fish, and rod catches should improve. Thankfully, too, fewer and fewer diseased fish are being seen. All this should mean that the Spey will remain one of the finest salmon rivers in Scotland. If you are lucky enough to be offered a day on any of its famous beats, don't think twice. Just say 'Yes'.

4. The Solway Rivers

The Border Esk

LOCATION:
Ordnance Survey Land Ranger Series, 1:50,000.
Sheets 85, Carlisle and Solway Firth, and 79,
Hawick and Eskdale.

GRID REFERENCES: Sheet 79, White Esk and Black Esk
confluence, 254908; Langholm, 365845; Canonbie, 394763;
Liddle Water, 398750; Longtown, 380686.

SEASONS: Salmon – February 1–October 31, with the best
runs in late summer. Trout – April 15–September 30. Best
months are during spring and summer.

FLIES: Salmon – Silver Doctor, General Practitioner, Logie,
Blue Charm, Hairy Mary. Trout – Peter Ross, March Brown,
Cinnamon and Gold, Teal and Silver, White Moth.

COSTS: A season ticket covering most waters will cost £320.
Prices per week vary from £10–£70 on Esk and Liddle
Fisheries Association waters.

PERMISSION: The Secretary, Esk and Liddle Fisheries
Association, Bank of Scotland Buildings, Langholm,
Dumfriesshire (Tel: 03873–80428). George Graham, Head
River-watcher, Hagg-on-Esk, Old School, Canonbie,
Dumfriesshire (Tel: 03873–71416). Mrs P Wylie,
Byreburnfoot, Canonbie, Dumfriesshire (Tel: 03873–71279).

THE BORDER ESK is a first-class sea-trout
river, and more than 5,000 fish are taken by
anglers in most seasons, some weighing 7 lb and
more. This 'dream water' begins at the confluence
of Black Esk and White Esk, at the foot of Castle
O'er Forest, and then winds seawards, gathering
in the waters of Meggat, Wauchope, Ewes,
Tarras, Liddle and Lyne before spilling over the
mud-flats into the Solway Firth.

For a mile, Esk forms the Border between
Scotland and England. The tributary Liddle then
takes on the role for 15 miles until its own little
feeder, Kershope Burn, takes over and carries the
Border line deep into Kielder Forest.
Afforestation on the upper reaches of the Esk
system as a whole has led to variable water levels,
and occasional flash floods and dry summers can
make the rivers virtually unfishable.

Fishing on parts of Esk and its tributaries are
controlled by the Esk and Liddle Fisheries
Association, on water owned by the Buccleuch
Estates. All angling has to be booked in advance
and no day tickets are available. The five beats
which make up this water account for more than
750 sea-trout in most years. In 1981 the catch was
a record 919.

Salmon also run the river, and the same beats
produced 48 fish in 1987. The average weight of
salmon is 10 lb, although heavier fish are not
uncommon. In 1988 one of 28 lb 8 oz was taken.
Salmon fry have been planted out in Esk
tributaries in recent years, and hopefully an
improvement in salmon-fishing will follow.

The upper reaches and tributaries of the Esk
provide exciting sport with wild brown trout.
They may run at only 8–12 oz, but the fun of
stalking them more than compensates for their
size. All you need is a short rod and a pair of good
climbing boots, and you can be alone for the day.

The Annan

LOCATION: Ordnance Survey Land Ranger Series, 1:50,000. **Sheets 78**, Nithsdale and Lowther Hills, and 85, Carlisle and Solway Firth.

GRID REFERENCES: Sheet 78, Devil's Beef Tub, 063128; Upper Annandale AA water, 099011. **Sheet 85**, Murraythwaite, 134734; Hoddom, 163727; Newbie, 195677.

SEASONS: Salmon – February 25–November 15, with the best sport in April and March, and September, October and November. Trout – March 15–October 6. The prime time is during summer.

FLIES: Salmon – Stoat's Tail, Munro Killer, Black Doctor, Thunder and Lightning, Blue Charm. Trout – Peter Ross, Teal and Silver, White Moth, Langholm Silver, March Brown, Cinnamon and Gold.

COSTS: A week's fishing on Annan will cost anything from £18 up to £210, depending on the beat and the time of season.

PERMISSION: Moffat: Upper Annandale Angling Association, J Black, 1 Rosehill Grange Road, Moffat, Dumfriesshire (Tel: 0683–20104).
Kinmount Estate: Hoddom and Hoddom Castle, Water Bailiff, Bridge Cottage, Hoddom, Dumfriesshire (Tel: 05763–488).
Castlemilk Estate: The Factor, Castlemilk Estate Office, Norwood, Lockerbie, Dumfriesshire (Tel: 05762–204).
Royal Four Towns: Clerk and Commissioners, Royal Four Towns Fishing, K Ratcliffe, Jay-Ar, Preston House Road, Hightae, Lockerbie, Dumfriesshire (Tel: 0387–220).
Halleaths Estate: Dryfeholm Water – Messers McJerrow and Stevenson, Solicitors, Lockerbie, Dumfriesshire (Tel: 05762–2123).
Hoddom Estate: Mrs Ward, Ecclefechan Hotel, Ecclefechan, Dumfriesshire.
Newbie Estate: Mr T Bayley, Water Bailiff, Newbie Mill Cottage, Annan, Dumfriesshire (Tel: 04612–2608).

RIVER ANNAN. An angler prepares for battle on Hoddam Water. Perhaps he will meet with one of the 30 lb salmon that frequent this river. Annan is better known for the quality of its sea-trout fishing, up to 1,000 are taken each season.

THE YOUNG ANNAN plunges down the slopes of the Devil's Beef Tub, not far from source of Tweed, and starts on a southerly course that takes it from hills carpeted with heather and deer grass to fertile lowland pastures.

Two miles south of Moffat, Annan gathers in Moffat Water and Evan Water, two tributaries that are far bigger than their parent river. From here, Annan flows lazily on to collect Kinnel Water, Dryfe Water, Water of Milk and Mein Water before swirling out into the Solway Firth below Annan Town. Naturally a spate river, it has benefitted from work to improve access to the spawning ground for migratory fish, which in turn is leading to a gradual improvement in sport.

Annan is divided into several beats, including Upper-Annandale Angling Association waters, Annandale Estate, Halleaths (famous for its deep, slow pools), Royal Four Towns, Murraythwaite, and Hoddom (Goat's and Kirkyard are noted pools here). The Newbie beats, above Annan Town, are timeshared, but occasional weeks and days are still available, and enquiry is worthwhile.

The main runs of sea-trout are in July, August and September, and about 1,000 are taken each season for an average of 2 lb. Salmon are caught mostly in the autumn, when some exceptionally heavy fish are taken, with 20-pounders coming regularly and fish of 30 lb-plus are not unknown. Brown trout are caught in the upper reaches, but most anglers are drawn by the excellent sea-trout fishing.

The Nith

LOCATION: Ordnance Survey Land Ranger Series, 1:50,000. **Sheets 70**, Ayr and Kilmarnock; 71, Lanark and Upper Nithsdale, 78, Nithsdale and Lowther Hills; and 84, Dumfries.

GRID REFERENCES: Sheet 71, House of Water, 551121; Sanquhar, 785095. **Sheet 78**, Buccleuch Estate Water, 858003; Thornhill, 875954; Barjarg, 885903. **Sheet 84**, Cairn, 986779; Burgh Water, 974771.

SEASONS: Salmon – February 25–November 30, with autumn best. Trout – March 15–October 6, with the best fishing in April, May and June.

FLIES: Salmon – Stoat's Tail, Munro Killer, Hairy Mary, Brown Turkey, Thunder and Lightning. Trout – Peter Ross, Black Pennell, Bloody Butcher, Teal and Silver, White Moth.

COSTS: Burgh Waters range from £45 for a week to £120 for a season. A week's fishing on Buccleuch Estate waters will cost from £115–£540, depending on time of season. Upper Nithsdale will cost between £30 and £60.

PERMISSION: Upper Nithsdale Angling Club: William Laidlaw, Water Bailiff, 22 Renwick Place, Sanquhar, Dumfriesshire (Tel: 0659–50612).
Buccleuch Estate: The Factor, Buccleuch Estates Ltd, Drumlanrig Mains, Thornhill, Dumfriesshire (Tel: 08486–283).
Buccleuch and Queensberry Hotel Water: Buccleuch and Queensberry Hotel, Thornhill, Dumfriesshire (Tel: 0848–30215).
Blackwood Estate: Smiths Gore, 28 Castle Street, Dumfries (Tel: 0387–63066).
Mid-Nithsdale Angling Association: Secretary, I Milligan, 123 Drumlanrig Street, Thornhill, Dumfriesshire (Tel: 0848–30555).
Dumfries and Galloway Angling Association: Secretary, D Conchie (Tel: 0387–55223).

Dumfries Burgh Water: Director of Finance, Nithsdale District Council, Municipal Chambers, Buccleuch Street, Dumfries (Tel: 0387–53166).

THE NITH IS the Solway's crowning. Its catches over recent years make it one of Scotland's finest salmon and sea-trout rivers.

Although spring salmon have virtually disappeared since the outbreak of UDN in 1967, runs of summer and autumn fish have been superb over recent seasons. Despite the occasional appearance of disease-marked fish in low water, and the problem of poaching, more than 10,000 migratory fish were caught in 1988.

The Nith is formed where Beoch Burn, Knockenlee Burn and their feeders come together at House of Water. From here, the river flows eastwards, gathering in other tributaries, with salmon fishing beginning in earnest around the little town of Sanquhar. Average annual catches of salmon on this 10-mile stretch of Nith are more than 450 salmon and grilse and 1,500 sea-trout.

The next four beats of Nith, above the little town of Thornhill, belong to Buccleuch Estates, but much fishing in and around Thornhill is controlled by the mid-Nithsdale Angling Association. Its waters yield more than 500 salmon and grilse and about the same number of sea-trout each year.

Beats from here to the estuary include Closeburn Castle, Barjarg, Blackwood, Friar's Carse, Ellisland Trust, Portrack and the Burgh Water in Dumfries. One of them, Barjarg, has a special claim to fame. In 1812, while the destruction of Napoleon's army was taking place, a poacher by the name of Jock Wallace had his own private battle. His triumph was the capture of a 67 lb salmon from the Barjarg stretch.

The Nith's main tributary, Cairn Water, is gathered in below Lincluden College. A Twelfth-century convent, it was later converted into a Collegiate Church.

RICH POOLS

Some of the best fishing on the Cairn is to be had in the small pools between Moniavie and Dunscore in the later months of the season, with rising or falling water the most productive. In summer drought it can become very weedy, with only a trickle of water. The Dumfries and Galloway Association sometimes puts a limit on the number of fish that may be caught.

In 1988, 430 salmon, 380 grilse and 200 sea-trout were caught, with the average weight of salmon at about 7 lb. The pool below Cluden Rock acts as a temperature barrier to fish, and the numbers of fish poached from here are unknown. Would the annual catch be doubled if poaching could be totally stopped? The bailiffs are having an uphill struggle with the poaching thugs, who now seem to be directing their underhand methods at fish and bailiffs alike.

Brown trout fishing is also good on the Cairn. In 1987, 3,500 were introduced, and subsequent catches have included trout of more than 2 lb, mostly to small flies. The bag-limit is eight trout a day, which many anglers achieve. Rainbow trout, escapees from fish-farms, are also caught.

Dumfries and Galloway Angling Association also planted out 10,000 sea-trout fry in the Cairn

in 1987, and it is hoped that future seasons will see increased numbers caught.

More than 4,000 salmon, 1,600 grilse and 4,500 sea-trout were grassed from Nith in 1988, with the salmon averaging about 9 lb, grilse about $5\frac{1}{2}$ lb, and sea-trout around 2 lb. The best months for salmon were September, October and November, and of the fish taken some weighed up to 30 lb.

The Burgh Water, centred in Dumfries, had excellent returns for 1988. An average of 20 salmon per day was caught in September and in June, 300 sea-trout were taken. The prime months for sea-trout are May, June and July. In 1988, June and July were the top months, with 1,200 and 1,500 caught respectively.

Dumfries Town has a cauld with a fish-ladder. Below this, in spring, excellent lies to try are Castledykes, Slae Bushes and Colonel's Wood. Upstream, large boulders have been placed in pools to create lies and to help deter poachers from netting. These boulders act as wonderful 'snags' to nets.

The Nith offers excellent salmon and sea-trout fishing at incredibly cheap prices. The Burgh Water was only £120 for the season in 1988. A weekly ticket at prime times cost £45. Nith is a river which deserves the attention of any seasoned angler.

The Cree

LOCATION: Ordnance Survey Land Ranger Series, 1:50,000. Sheets 76, Girvan; 77, New Galloway and Glen Trool; and 83, Kirkcudbright.

GRID REFERENCES: Sheet 76, Loch Moan, 343855; Birch Linn, 331770. **Sheet 77,** Water of Troll and Minnoch confluence, 376779; Trool and Cree confluence, 358744. **Sheet 83,** Galloway Estate, 387677; Newton Stewart, 407655.

SEASONS: Salmon – March 1–October 14, with best runs in autumn. Trout – March 15–October 6, with June and July the prime months.

FLIES: Salmon – Blue Charm, Silver Stoat, Dunkeld, Yellow Dog, Hairy Mary. Trout – Grouse and Claret, Cinnamon and Gold, Silver Butcher, Black Pennell, Peter Ross.

COSTS: A week's fishing for three rods on Galloway Estate water, including gillie, will cost £550 in the autumn. Earlier weeks may be had for £120. Association waters will cost £8 per rod per day.

PERMISSION: Galloway Estate: Mrs J Robb, G M Thomson and Co, Victoria Street, Newton Stewart, Wigtownshire (Tel: 0671–2887).
Drumlamford Estate: A McKeand, Drumlamford Estate, Barrhill, Ayrshire (Tel: 046582–256).
Newton Stewart Angligh Association: Newton Stewart Angling Association, D G Guns and Tackle, 32 Albert Street, Newton Stewart, Wigtownshire (Tel: 0671–3224).

RIVER CREE. Best salmon fishing is on the Galloway Estate. Here the river meanders lazily through fertile pastures, her soil banks graced with leafy trees. Upwards of 100 salmon are taken from this stretch each season.

CREE AND BLADNOCH are usually considered together, under that heading, since both spill over Wigtown Sands and at low tide their waters share a common channel into Wigtown Bay and the Solway Firth.

The Cree rises from Loch Moan, deep in Glentrool Forest, where the dark conspiracy of conifers hides its waters for the first nine miles. It eventual'y shakes away the forest as it splashes over Birch Linn waterfall and passes through open, boggy moorlands for a couple of miles before Glentrool's trees close in once more. Also flowing from the forest are the two main tributaries, Water of Trool and Water of Minnoch.

No sooner does Cree finally escape the forest than it meanders reluctantly into Newton Stewart and on to Wigtown Sands to meet with the Bladnoch. At the estuary can be seen the rotting remains of timber stakes once used, with brushwood, to net salmon.

Sea-trout entering the Cree tend to head for the lower feeder burns to spawn. If you fish the tidal reaches, remember that their mouths will be still be soft from feeding at sea.

The Cree's best salmon-fishing is on the Galloway Estate water. The three beats begin above Newton Stewart and extend upstream for about five miles. Each season around 120 salmon are taken, most of them in October. These three beats are offered on a timeshare basis (one week for three years) or on a weekly-let basis.

RIVER BLADNOCH. A lady angler trys on the last days of the season to catch a salmon. Recent rain has helped raise the river level, a gentle breeze and overcast skies make her chances good.

The Bladnoch

LOCATION: Ordnance Survey Land Ranger Series, 1:50,000. Sheets 76, Girvan; 82, Stranraer and Glen Luce; and 83, Kirkcudbright.

GRID REFERENCES: Sheet 76, Loch Maberry, 285755; Tarf and Bladnoch Junction, 348604. **Sheet 83**, Mochrum park, 363572; High Barness, 385545; Low Barness, 394554; Bladnoch Town, 422543.

SEASONS: Salmon – February 14–October 31, with September and October best. Trout – March 15–October 6.

FLIES: Salmon – Blue Charm, Dunkeld, Stoat's Tail, Yellow Dog, Garry Dog. Trout – White Moth, Peter Ross, March Brown, Silver Butcher, Teal and Silver.

COSTS: £50 per rod per week for prime months on Barness Waters. Accommodation is available in cottages on the estate, these sleep two to four people and cost £100–£200 per week depending on the time of season. Other Bladnoch Waters will cost between £8 and £11 per day.

PERMISSION: Mochrum Park, Barness: Hayley, Foxen Lanehead Hall, Soyland, Ripponend, Yorkshire (Tel: 0422–822148 or 60434).
Corsemalzie: Corsemalzie House Hotel, Port William, Newtown Stewart, Wigtownshire (Tel: 0988–86254).
Association Water: Newton Stewart Angling Association, Galloway Guns and Tackle, Albert Street, Newton Stewart, Wigtownshire (Tel: 0671–3224).

THE BLADNOCH HAS its beginnings high on Darnarroch Fell (235 m), collecting in feeder burns and loch waters which flow as Pulganny Burn into Loch Maberry. From here to the estuary the river meanders through marshlands, its banks liable to flooding in times of heavy rain, and its twisting, weaving course causing it almost to double back on itself.

The biggest tributary is Tarf Water, an excellent trout and salmon river which is gathered in at the front of sedge-covered Boreland Fell (90 m). The best runs of salmon on Tarf are in autumn when sport can be fast and furious, but spring can also bring some good runs both here and on Bladnoch itself. Sea-trout fishing is secondary to the superb salmon and trout fishing.

Bladnoch is stocked annually with brown trout of up to 1 lb, and trout to more than 3 lb are not uncommon. Be sure to check what you have hooked.

Salmon beats not to be missed are Mochrum Park, High and Low Barness and Corsemalzie. But book in advance. The Bladnoch is becoming a first-class river and better-known now that the estuary nets are gradually being bought-out.

The Bladnoch ends its 21-mile course when it flows into West Channel, at its confluence with the Cree.

RIVER BLADNOCH. Salmon and anglers alike are patiently waiting for autumn rains to raise water levels after the long summer drought of 1989. Earlier months see fishermen in search of brown trout. 3 lb specimens are not uncommon.

5. The Northern Isles

Orkney

LOCATION: Ordnance Survey Second Series, 1:50,000. Sheets 5, Orkney – Northern Isles; 6, Orkney – Mainland; and 7, Pentland Firth.

GRID REFERENCES: Sheet 6, Loch Boardhouse, 270260; Loch of Harray, 300140; Loch of Hundland, 295260; Loch of Stenness, 280130; Loch of Swannay, 310280.

SEASONS: Sea-trout – February 25–October 31. Brown trout – March 15–September 30.

FLIES: Same for sea-trout and brown trout – Black Pennell, Black Zulu, Blue Zulu, Ke-He, Loch Ordie, Soldier Palmer, Invicta, March Brown, Greenwell's Glory, Grouse and Green, Grouse and Claret, Green Peter, Bibio, Woodcock and Hare-lug, Silver Invicta, Dunkeld, Alexandra, Peter Ross, Bloody Butcher, Silver Butcher, Hardy's Gold Butcher.

COSTS: Theoretically free of charge, but most anglers join the Orkney Anglers' Association. The charge is modest, being less than £10.

CONTACT: The Secretary, Orkney Trout Fishing Association, c/o Orkney Tourist Board, 6 Broad Street, Kirkwall (Tel: 0856–2856).

ORKNEY WAS UNTIL 1468 part of the Kingdom of Denmark and Norway, the last remnant of Viking rule in Scotland. King Christian pledged the islands as security for part of the dowry of his daughter, Margaret, but the 12-year-old princess married 18-year-old King James III in July, 1469, at Holyrood Abbey in Edinburgh, and the pledge was never redeemed. As a result, Orkney, and King Christian's rights in Shetland, remained with the Scottish Crown.

The islands lie six miles across the broken waters of the Pentland Firth from Caithness on mainland Scotland. They are serviced by regular ferries from Scrabster Harbour, Thurso, a foot-passenger boat from John O'Groats, and regular air services from Wick and Aberdeen. There are plans for a new car-ferry, due to be operational in 1990.

The sea approach to Orkney into Stromness, is dominated by the island of Hoy, with its dramatic, red cliffs, peaked by Ward Hill (481 m), the highest point on Orkney. Hoy forms the western boundary of Scapa Flow, and good sea-trout fishing can be had along its sheltered north shore.

In 1989, Ian Hutcheon had excellent catches of sea-trout from the Evie Shore, taking fish of up to 3 lb on several occasions; and the Orkney Trout Fishing Association is actively improving sea-trout stocks with hatchery-bred native fish.

Sea-trout may also be encountered in the Bay of Firth, Isbister and Deer Sound, and along the Rendall Shore. Other favourite locations are near Finstown Brig and Inganess. Catching these great sporting fish in the sea is considered by many to be the pinnacle of angling pleasure.

Mainland Orkney is a complete contrast to the wild island of Hoy. The land is fertile and well farmed, graced by fine cattle and sheep, with good crops of barley and potatoes. Kirkwall, with its beautiful St Magnus cathedral, is the main population centre; a thriving, busy, cosmopolitan town.

Orkney has been home and haven for travellers for thousands of years, and few places have a greater concentration of ancient monuments. The most dramatic are the Standing Stones of Stenness and the Ring of Brodgar,

LOCH OF HARRAY. Outboards attached, rods assembled, casts tied, then lets begin the International Fly Fishing Championship. Conditions are superb, a gentle breeze ruffles the surface. May the best team win.

which stand between the islands' two principal lochs, Loch of Stenness and Loch of Harray. Close by is a chambered cairn, hewn from Orkney flagstone nearly 5,000 years ago.

But Orkney's most famous monument, Skara Brae, is a perfectly preserved neolithic village, hidden for centuries under sand dunes at the Bay of Skail. Even pieces of 'furniture' have survived, including a stone seat, hearth, box beds, dressers, two shelves and wall-cupboards.

The early settlers no doubt relied largely on fish for their food; and now, as then, Orkney has an abundance of fishing of great quality, easily accessible and readily available to the visiting angler.

Orkney mainland has five principal brown-trout lochs: Stenness, Harray, Swannay, Boardhouse and Hundland. A number of smaller waters are scattered about both Mainland and the surrounding islands, but the quality of sport on these five waters makes them the key objective of most visiting anglers.

QUALITY AND SPORT

Loch of Stenness produces brown trout of outstanding quality, among them, some years ago, a fish weighing 29 lb, one of the heaviest trout ever caught in Britain.

Sea-trout can also be caught in Loch of Stenness and at times in Loch of Harray, which connects with it. However, Harray, the largest Orkney water, is better known for its brown trout and has produced a real, 'glass-case' fish, a trout weighing 17 lb 8 oz and caught in 1964. Sample baskets taken by Harray anglers highlight the quality of fishing: in 1989 Ivor Simpson had a basket of 46 trout weighing 40 lb; two anglers fishing Harray and Stenness had 137 fish for 130 lb 4 oz.

In August, 1989, after high tides washed into Harray, raising its level, a fine sea-trout of 5 lb 5 oz was landed in the Biggings area by an angler fishing with a Black Zulu.

Loch of Hundland and Loch of Boardhouse, joined by a small burn, can both provide spectacular sport. Boardhouse produced two lovely fish one summer evening for a local angler during 1989: one weighing 3 lb 9 oz, the other 3 lb 4 oz. Both were taken on a Loch Ordie.

Loch of Hundland is stocked by the Orkney Trout Fishing Association and has a reputation for being dour. However, on its day, little Hundland can be very rewarding and it is always worth a cast.

The last loch, Swannay, is reputed by many local fisherman to be the jewel in Orkney's angling crown. Swannay lies on the north of Mainland and is a shallow, often windy water, where trout average 1 lb and fight like fish of twice that size.

Before you set out to sample the joys of Orkney fishing, your first port of call should be Sinclair's Tackle Shop in Stromness, close to the ferry berth. There you may join the Orkney Trout Fishing Association. It deserves the support of every visiting angler and by becoming a member you will obtain the use of the club's premises and facilities, and help to preserve, protect and improve Orkney gamefishing for the pleasure and enjoyment of future generations.

Shetland

LOCATION: Ordnance Survey Second Series, 1:50,000. Sheets 1, Shetland – Yell and Unst; 2, Shetland – Whalsay; 3, Shetland – North Mainland; and 4, Shetland – South Mainland.

GRID REFERENCES: Sheet 1, Loch of Snarravoe, 570016. **Sheet 2**, Loch of Huxter, 558623; Tonga Water, 333875. **Sheet 3**, Loch of Girlsta, 435520; Loch of Benston, 462535. **Sheet 4**, Loch of Tingwall, 414425.

SEASONS: As for Orkney.

FLIES: As for Orkney.

COSTS: Theoretically free of charge, but most visitors join the Shetland Anglers' Association. Its charges are modest, being less than £10.

CONTACT: The Secretary, Shetland Anglers' Association, 3 Gladstone Terrace, Lerwick (Tel: 0595-3729). The Secretary, Whalsay Anglers' Association, 3 Saeter, Symbister, Whalsay (Tel: 08066-472). The Secretary, Yell Anglers' Association, Gairdie, Mid Yell (Tel: 0957-2204). The Secretary, Unst Anglers' Association, Beltersound, Unst.

SHETLAND. Visiting anglers to these islands are faced with the dilemma of where to start. Advice should be sought from the Shetland Anglers' Association in Lerwick. An added bonus for anglers is the absence of midges from these islands.

THE SHETLAND ISLES extend over an area of 550 square miles and lie closer to Norway than they do to mainland Scotland. The principal islands are Mainland, Whalsay, Yell, Fetlar and Unst; and each offers excellent gamefishing opportunities for the visiting angler.

People have been visiting Shetland for thousands of years, and the memorials of their passing lie scattered throughout the isles; wonderfully preserved, early settlements such as Jarlshof, which shows evidence of continuous occupation from 4,500 years ago, through the Bronze Age and Iron Age down to Viking times.

The islands have chambered tombs, standing stones and cairns, hill forts and brochs, of the last, the best preserved is Mousa Broch, standing on an island made of flagstone. It is 50 ft in diameter its walls are some 43 ft 6 in high. Hundreds of these ancient defensive towers were built throughout the north from about 200 BC to 200AD, but Mousa Broch is the most outstanding example.

Fishing was, and still is (although to a lesser extent) a serious business in Shetland. Fish were the staple diet before the introduction of potatoes, and gutted fish were salted and hung up to dry in the smoke from the croft fires. Fish-oil was used to light lamps.

The crofters' diet was supplemented with gulls' eggs, collected dangerously from sheer, wave-lashed cliffs. Fertile land is a sparse commodity on Shetland, and fields are small continuously wind-swept and difficult to work.

Whaling and herring fishing used to provide temporary jobs; during summer, men would sign onto a boat and go off to the South Atlantic, leaving youngsters and women to tend the crofts.

Women worked also in the herring stations,

gutting and salting fish and packing them into barrels. At the height of the Shetland herring industry, in 1907,457,034 barrels were cured and exported from Shetland and, a fleet of 40 boats operated from Aith Voe, to the east of Lerwick.

Nowadays, visiting fishermen are looking mostly for trout, and they have hundreds of lochs from which to choose all containing natural stocks of good-quality wild brown trout, varying from a few ounces up to fish of 8 lb or more. Well, almost all: Loch of Garth and Kirk Loch on Yell are fishless. But they are very much the exceptions on Shetland.

Shetland is famous for the quality of its sea-trout fishing, although for reasons best known to themselves, salmon tend to pass by the islands. Recent years have seen declining runs of sea-trout as elsewhere in Scotland, and in Ireland, but they are still there and the Shetland anglers' speciality is catching these superb, sporting fish actually in the sea as they shoal up the narrow, finger-like fjords or voes.

WALKING COUNTRY

Deciding where to go is the most difficult problem facing a visiting angler, but the best place to start is at the Shetland Anglers' Association clubhouse in Lerwick, where, for a modest fee, you may purchase a visitor's ticket giving access to the club's waters – which means most of the lochs on the islands. In addition, the association publishes an excellent guide to its waters, including details of the most popular sea-trout fishing locations along the coast and in the voes.

Shetland has a wide variety of brown-trout waters to suit anglers of all degrees of physical fitness and fishing ability: lochs where you are

assured of fun with small, bright little trout; others, at the end of a long, tiring, moorland walk, which may reward you with a fish of more than 4 lb. All will delight.

Loch of Tingwall, a few miles west of Lerwick, is one of the best of the Shetland lochs. It is carefully managed by the association and regularly stocked with native-bred fish; the water is lime-rich and provides excellent feeding. The fish grow rapidly and are of superb quality.

Another first-class water is Loch of Benston, to the north or Lerwick, where trout average 1 lb 8 oz and fish of more than 3 lb are taken most seasons. Benston is a delightful loch, surrounded by green fields and wild hills. Both boat and bank fishing is allowed.

Loch of Girlsta, named after a Norwegian princess who is reputed to have drowned in the loch, is a long, dour, deep, windy water; but it holds some outstanding fish. The heaviest brown trout ever caught in Shetland, a fish of 12 lb 8 oz, was taken from Girlsta. But wading is dangerous on Girlsta, and unless you have been given a full briefing from a local angler, or, better still have his company, keep off the water. In any case, boat-fishing brings best results, but here again, take great care: Girlsta really catches the wind and can become very rough very quickly.

The outer islands also offer good sport and are easy to reach, because Shetland has a good inter-island ferry service. Whalsay has three excellent lochs, including Loch of Huxter, where a trout of 9 lb 9 oz was caught in 1983.

Unst has good sea-trout fishing, particularly at Dales Voe and Weisdale and Burra Firth at the north of the island; with good brown trout fishing on Loch of Cliff and Loch Snarravoe, which is

stocked with a Loch Leven strain of fish.

Yell also has productive sea-trout fishing during autumn, and sport with brown trout on Lochs Papil and Cullivoe. Tiny Fetlar boasts three lochs where good sport may be had, and the chance of seeing that most famous of all Shetland birds, the snowy owl.

For the angler who likes a good walk to his fishing, Shetland is a dream come true. Moorlands are scattered with dozens of fine waters, and the wildlife along the way is spectacular: tumbling Arctic Skua, piping golden plover, great skua, and always the chance of meeting an otter.

Ronas Hill, on Mainland, is the highest point in Shetland. From the summit a magnificent view awaits, a vast panorama of sunlight, sea and sky; and below, sparkling like silver raindrops, a wonderful series of five trout waters: Birka, Many Crooks, Tonga Water, Roer Water and many more.

Shetland offers perhaps the finest, value-for-money fishing in Scotland, amid some of Scotland's most lovely scenery. And there's a bonus: no midges. Midges can't survive in a wind of more than 5 mph, and on Shetland a speed less than that is something of a rarity.

RIVER SPEY. Looking downstream from the bridge at Marypark. A wet autumn ensured that a lot of fish were able to make it to their spawning grounds. An excellent omen for the forthcoming season, 1990.

Above

RIVER NITH. A last salmon of the season for this angler. Taken four and a half miles north of Dumfries near Auldgirth. No other Scottish river can boast returns of over 10,000 migratory fish, available to anglers from only £45.00 per week.

Left

RIVER TAY. The waters around Dunkeld give anglers salmon over 30 lb every season. On opening day of the 1990 season Ian Watson caught a 10 lb specimen. Lets hope this is a good omen for the rest of the season is as productive.

No FISHING career is complete without a visit to Orkney. The best fishing is on the mainland. It is a perfect place to base your holiday. One of the heaviest British brown trout caught was a 29 lb specimen from Loch of Stenness.

River border Esk. A beautiful late autumn afternoon near Canonbie. It is arguably Scotlands finest sea-trout water, upwards of 5,000 are caught each season. It is wise to book well in advance as Esk fishing is much sought after in prime months.

RIVER EWE. Linkin[g]
famous Loch Ma[...]
to the sea is River Ew[e]
Only a mile in length,
takes little time under
normal conditions for
sea-trout and salmon
run up. Spurred on in
their efforts by the gre[at]
seals which frequent
these waters as well.

6. The Tay

LOCATION: Ordnance Survey Land Ranger Series, 1:50,000. Sheets 51, Loch Tay; 52, Aberfeldy and Glen Almond; 53, Blairgowrie; and 58, Perth and Kinross.

GRID REFERENCES: Sheet 51, Falls of Dochart, 570323; Lyon Junction Pool 793478. **Sheet 52**, Tummel Junction Pool, 977513; Dunkeld, 026426; Glendelvine, 070405. **Sheet 53**, Caputh 089400; Kercock, 128387; Meikleour, 155386; Islamouth Junction, 158375; Cargill, 152369; Campsie Linn 124340; Taymount House, 123342; Stanley, 123327; Redgorton, 097283; Scone Palace, 115268.

SEASONS: Salmon – January 15–October 15. The best months on Loch Tay are from January to May. Prime months on the river are from September to the end of October. January through to May can also produce good fishing. Trout – March 15–October 6, with the best fishing from late May to the end of June.

FLIES: Salmon – Blue Charm, Hairy Mary, Stoat's Tail, Munro Killer, Garry Dog, Silver Wilkinson, General Practitioner. Trout – Invicta, Black Spider, Wickham's Fancy, Silver Butcher, Black Pennell.

LURES FOR SALMON: Yellow-belly, Devon, Toby, Kynoch Killer, Rapala.

COSTS: The cost of Tay fishing varies widely. The Loch Tay offers a wide selection of excellent accommodation to suit virtually any budget. The fishing may cost as little as £8 per rod a day. The upper reaches of the Tay also represent excellent value for money, with costs from £8. Middle Tay fishing is still within reach of many people, with prices from as little as £15 per day up to £35, depending on the time of season. The cream of Tay fishing on the lower reaches will cost anything up to £300 per rod per day in autumn.

INFORMATION: The Perthshire Tourist Board, PO Box 33, George Inn Lane, Perth (Tel: 0738–27958), will supply details of accommodation on Tayside and suggest excursions for non-fishing visitors.

PERMISSION: Loch Tay: Ardeonaig Hotel, Killin, Perthshire (Tel; 0567–2249).
Loch Tay: Clachgaig Hotel, Killin, Perthshire (Tel: 0567–2270).
Loch Tay: Killin Hotel, Killin, Perthshire (Tel: 0567–2296).
Loch Tay: Highland Lodges, Milton Moornish, Killin Perthshire (Tel: 0567–2323).
Loch Tay: Kenmore Hotel, Aberfeldy, Perthshire (Tel: 0887–3205).
Loch Tay: Croft-na-Caber, Guest House, South Loch Road, Kenmore, Perthshire (Tel: 0887–3236).

Loch Tay: Ben Lawers Hotel, Lawers, Aberfeldy, Perthshire (Tel: 0567–2436).
Dochart and Lochay: D & S Allen Tackle-dealers, Main Street, Killin, Perthshire (Tel: 0567–2362).
Kenmore: Kenmore Hotel, Aberfeldy, Perthshire (Tel: 08873–205).
Lyon: Finlayson Hughes Estate Office, Aberfeldy, Perthshire (Tel: 0887–29004).
Lyon: Fortingall Hotel, Fortingall, Aberfeldy, Perthshire (Tel: 08873–367).
Farleyer: Major N Ramsey, Farleyer, Aberfeldy, Perthshire (Tel: 0887–20540).
Weem: Weem Hotel, Weem, by Aberfeldy, Perthshire (Tel: 0887–20381).
Aberfeldy: Aberfeldy Angling Club, The Secretary, 65 Moness Cresent, Aberfeldy, Perthshire, (Tel: 0887–20488).
Aberfeldy and District: Finlayson Hughes, Estates Office, Aberfeldy, Perthshire (Tel: 0887–20904).
Grandtully and Logierait: Mrs J Grey, Mill of Logierait, Pitlochry, Perthshire (Tel: 0796–230).
Grandtully: Grandtully Hotel, Strathtay, Perthshire (Tel: 08874–207).
Edradynate: Mrs B Campbell, Strathtay, Perthshire (Tel: 08874–359).
Derculich, Fyndynate and Killieschassie: Finalyson Hughes, Estate Office, Aberfeldy, Perthshire (Tel: 0887–20904).
Kinnaird: Savills, Chartered Surveyors, Brechin, Angus (Tel: 03562–2187).
Tummel: Pitlochry Tourist Information Office, 22 Atholl Road, Pitlochry, Perthshire (Tel: 0796–2215).
Garry: Atholl Estates, Estates Office, Blair Atholl, Perthshire (Tel: 079681–355).
Ballinluig: Logierait Hotel, Ballinluig, Perthshire (Tel: 0796–82253).
Dalguise: Mr M C Smith, Burnside, Dalguise, Dunkeld, Perthshire (Tel: 03502–593).
Dunkeld: Stakis Dunkeld House Hotel, Dunkeld, Perthshire (Tel: 03502–771).

Dunkeld: Nick Hodgkinson, St Ninian's Wynd, Dunkeld, Perthshire (Tel: 03502–8861).
Newtyle: Mrs E Redford, Holmlea, Station Road, Errol, Perthshire (Tel: 08212–312).
Glendelvine: Glendelvine Estate Office, Glendelvine, Perthshire (Tel: 0738–71276).
Murthly: Murthly and Strathbraan Estate Office, Douglasfield, Murthly, by Dunkeld, Perthshire (Tel: 0738–71480).
Delvine, Upper and Lower Kercock: Finlayson Hughes, 29 Barrossa Place, Perth (Tel: 0738–30926).
Meikleour: Meikleour Sporting Estate Office, Meikleour, Perth (Tel: 025083–210).
Isla and Ericht: James Crockart and Sons, 26–28 Allan Street, Blairgowrie, Perthshire (Tel: 0250–2056).
Lower Tay: Bell–Ingram, Durn, Isla Road, Perth (Tel: 0738–21121).
Ballathie: Ballathie Estates Office, Ballathie Farms, Balmains, Stanley, Perth (Tel: 0738–82250).
Taymount: Taymount House, Stanley, Perth (Tel: 0738–828203).
Stanley: Tayside Hotel, Stanley, Perth (Tel: 0738–82249).
Scone: Scone Estate Office, Scone Palace, Perth (Tel: 0738–52038).
Perth: Director of Finance, District Council Chambers, High Street, Perth (Tel: 0738–39911).

THE TAY IS arguably Scotland's most revered salmon river. Its 114-mile journey begins amid the mountains of the Argyll Perthshire border and ends between the fertile banks of its firth, downstream of Perth.

At the head of the main river is Loch Tay, fed by the Dochart and Lochay, The Dochart is the true mother of Tay, gathering its streams from the slopes of Ben Lui (1,128 m), awash with heather and bog myrtle. These burns come together to flow first as Fillan Water, hurrying past Crianlarich and on into Loch Dochart. On an island in the loch are remains of Dochart Castle, built to guard the narrow pass into the glen.

Flowing east from the loch, the river is joined by the Benmore Burn, tumbling over itself in its wild rush from the slopes of Ben More, (1,174 m), Stob Binnein (1,165 m), and Stob Garbh (960 m). Its waters swell the Dochart as it meanders through boggy ground before Loch Iubhair, the northern banks of which are littered with lichen-encrusted crags.

Eastwards from the loch, the true Dochart scurries down the glen to surge over the magnificent Falls of Dochart at Killin. Salmon do not usually reach this far upstream until water temperatures have risen sufficiently, normally in mid-May, but the best fishing is in late summer and autumn. Salmon caught here have usually been in fresh water for at least a month, and their condition reflects that fact. But in 1989, following an exceptionally mild winter, with temperatures seldom falling below 40 degrees Fahrenheit, the fish had a quick passage up river and arrived in these upper reaches still comparatively fresh.

Killin, below the frowning Sron a' Chlachain (521 m), lies on the westernmost shore of Loch Tay. In the Mill of Killin are eight stones, said to have been owned by St Fillian, who lived and worked in and around Glen Dochart in the early days of Christianity. Each of the stones supposedly contains healing properties for different parts of the body.

Below Killin, Dochart is joined first by many burns and then by the Lochay, its waters tapped for generating hydro-electricity. Salmon ladders take the fish up the falls, to the upper river and the spawning reeds.

Loch Tay is more than 14 miles long, three-quarters of a mile wide and more than 450 ft deep. The average weight of its brown trout is around $\frac{3}{4}$ lb, but fish to more than 5 lb are taken. The loch also holds rainbow trout, escapees from cages and a menace to the salmon fry and smolts. The shallow areas of the loch's east and west ends are the best fishing areas, but a gillie who knows the lies is an essential boat companion. The average weight of Loch Tay salmon is about 17 lb. They are taken mostly in the spring and mostly by trolling.

SPECTACULAR SCENERY

When fishing the loch's western reaches, glance up at the ruins of Finlarig Castle, once the seat of the notorious Black Duncan, Earl of Orchy. The best-preserved parts of the castle are the dungeons and beheading pit. Black Duncan is said to have made full use of them.

Standing guard over Loch Tay's northern edge is Ben Lawers (1,214 m). From its summit, on clear days, you can see both east and west coasts. Its slopes are a botanist's paradise, with mosses and lichens found nowhere else in the British Isles. One rocky ledge boasts moss campion, Alpine forget-me-not and mossy cyphel all competing for a place on the thin, mineral-rich soil.

With an improved salmon run into the Lochay, and the buying-out of nets downstream, prospects for future salmon fishing on the loch are becoming brighter. Loch Tayside has several good hotels with fishing rights ideally situated for an angling holiday amid spectacular scenery.

At the eastern end of the loch is Kenmore

R IVER TAY. The waters around Dunkeld give anglers salmon over 30 lb every season. On opening day of the 1990 season Ian Watson caught a 10 lb specimen. Lets hope this is a good omen for the rest of the season.

A day for five rods on Islamouth itself in October will cost about £950. The cheapest Victoria stayed at Taymouth on her first visit to the Highlands in 1842, her host, Lord Breadalbane, who had mined the surrounding hills for gold and copper.

The first beats on the Tay are controlled by Kenmore Hotel, where, each January 15, the breaking of a bottle of whisky over the bows of one of the hotel boats marks the opening of a new season after the first fishermen have been piped to the water's edge. Much of the fishing on the Tay is from boats. It's a big, fast river with deep pools and the banks are often too wooded to allow easy casting from the banks. Wading is often not advisable.

The Kenmore water finishes at the junction with the Lyon, one of the biggest tributaries of the Tay. Like Lochay, this river has been affected by a hydro-electric scheme, with a dam built at Lubreach at the end of Loch Lyon. This resulted in an increase in water depth of around 60 ft and stopped salmon reaching the upstream spawning grounds. The main spawning is now in the lower river and its small tributaries. The best fishing on the Lyon is for about seven miles upstream from its confluence with the Tay.

It is an exciting river to fish, with falls and white water into deep, dark pools. The river's pace eases only in its last two miles to the Tay. Waters are drawn from the wild and turbulent moorlands of South Rannoch, which collect in Loch Lyon behind the Hydro-electric dam, and are now inaccessible to migratory fish.

Glen Lyon is most beautiful in autumn, with its trees turning gold, red and brown. The gorge the river has cut is so narrow in places that you

Notable catches on the Tay

WEIGHT	ANGLER	LOCATION	WEIGHT	ANGLER	LOCATION
38 lb	Kenneth Gregory	Dunkeld	26 lb	Mr Miller	Stanley
35 lb	Terry Roberts	Ballathie	26 lb	Gordon Clapperton	Logierait
34 lb	Bob Campbell	Stobhall	26 lb	George McInnes	Stobhall
34 lb	Michael Smith	Kinnaird	26 lb	Mr Fox	Dunkeld
34 lb	Mr Williams	Dunkeld	25 lb 8 oz	Raymond Janetta	Loch Tay
34 lb	Ian Ferguson	Stormont	25 lb	Lex Brown	Kinnaird
34 lb	Dan McGinty	Taymount	25 lb	Hugh Law	Redgorton
33 lb 8 oz	Francois Steven	Redgorton	25 lb	Mr H Snell	Redgorton
30 lb 12 oz	Charles Whyte	Scone	24 lb	Sylvia Marshall	Murthly
30 lb	Mr Surridge	Perth	24 lb	Gordon Patterson	Perth
30 lb	Mr Lloyd	Dunkeld	23 lb	Frank Fyne	Taymount
29 lb 8 oz	Mrs Jarvis	Taymount	23 lb	Alistair Nicoll	Murthly
29 lb	Mr Woods	Stobhall	23 lb	Peter Thomas	Scone
29 lb	Lex Brown	Kinnaird	23 lb	Kenneth Gregory	Dunkeld
29 lb	David Henderson	Dunkeld	23 lb	Alastair McGregor	Almondmouth
28 lb 8 oz	Ken Thomas	Scone	23 lb	Mr Ridgeway	Murthly
28 lb 8 oz	George Gartshore	Loch Tay	22 lb	Dr I Oglesby	Dalguise
28 lb	Brian Marshall	Newtyle	22 lb	Mr Williams	Farleyer
28 lb	Ian Porter	Scone	22 lb	John Frazier	Kenmore
28 lb	Fred Barclay	Taymount	22 lb	Ken Bell	Dunkeld
28 lb	Chapman Pincher	Kinnaird	21 lb 8 oz	Mr Malone	Farleyer
27 lb 8 oz	Ian McLaren	Logierait			
27 lb 8 oz	Mr Garnett	Islamouth			
27 lb 8 oz	Mrs Jarvis	Taymount			
27 lb 8 oz	Barry Oldham	Scone			
27 lb	Geoff Duke	Taymount			
27 lb	Steven McGirven	Glendelvine			
27 lb	Mr Clelland	Islamouth			
27 lb	Robert McIntyre	Kenmore			
26 lb	Frank Fyne	Taymount			

village, built to house people out of sight of their chief, who lived in Taymouth Castle. Queen MacGregor of Glenstrae, who was hunted down by Clan Campbell after he had revenged two MacGregor murders in 1565. He is said to have leapt the gorge to escape from his pursuers.

Late season is also a prime time for fishing, but fresh-run spring salmon of 17–20 lb are occasionally caught on the lower river. Recent years have seen Lyon much improved, with work done to break up impacted gravel and thus improve the spawning grounds. Several thousand fry have been planted out. The river has a wealth of pools, with some of the most attractive on the Fortingall water. In the local church-yard is a 3,000-year-old yew, said to be the most ancient tree in Europe.

Back on the Tay, from Lyon junction almost to Aberfeldy are the Farleyer and Bolfracks beats. The low ground on either bank is scattered with pictish cairns and standing stones, and at Aberfeldy, General Wade's Military Road crosses the river. Aberfeldy Bridge, built in 1733, is the finest example of Wade's attempt to keep open his lines of communication between the Highlands and Lowlands.

It was here that the Black Watch first gathered as a fighting force when war with Spain broke out in 1740. Previously it had been used only to keep peace among the hot-tempered Highlanders. Non particularly wanted to fight abroad, and the regiment was force-marched to London, supposedly to be reviewed by the King. Once there, they were told they were going to the West Indies. A few deserted, and three of those caught were shot in the Tower of London.

So the regiment went to war, and within months, at the battle of Fontenoy, it had won its first honours and its fame had begun. It was argued that by forcing the Black Watch abroad, the Government increased support for the 1745 rebellion.

On the other side of Aberfeldy Bridge is the village of Weem, which lends its name to the next stretch of the Tay. Its sixteenth-century church contains graves of the Menzies, who moved to the area in 1266. Their first Castle Menzies was burnt down by a descendant of the notorious Wolf of Badenoch in 1502. It was rebuilt, but is now in decay, though Clan Menzies are restoring it. The Castle gained fame as a refuge for the retreating Scottish darling, Bonnie Prince Charlie, after the failure of the 1745 rebellion. It was James Menzies who was credited with introducing larch trees to Scotland. They were planted at Taymouth in 1738.

It is at Aberfeldy Water that the Tay is joined by Urlar Burn, with its beautiful Falls of Moness, thundering down from craggy, heather-clad Meall a' Choire Chreagaich (665 m).

From here down to the estuary, the river is constantly changing course and cutting ox-bows out of surrounding fertile pastures, hugged by alder, hazel and willow. But first a few miles down, after flowing through beats such as Edradynate and Grandtully it makes a long, graceful curve to head south into Strathmore and to swallow up the Tummel at Logierait.

The Tummel and its main tributary, the Perthshire Garry, have been harnessed for hydro-electric schemes, resulting in salmon spawning grounds being lost and parts of the Garry running virtually dry. Salmon are still caught, and in 1989 they included a 31-pounder but the magnificent days of old are gone forever.

The best time to fish the upper Tay is from opening day through to May. All the upriver fishings have improved since the weir at Stanley was altered to allow salmon better access upstream. The weir formerly created a temperature pool, holding the fish back.

Much of the Tay has wooded banks, and at Dunkeld, the conifers surrounding Dunkeld House are said to be more than 200 years old. In Dunkeld, with its Cathedral Church of St Columba, the river is joined by the Braan. The Black Linn, the acclaimed falls of Braan, is impossable to salmon.

In the ninth century Dunkeld became the religous centre of Scotland with the unification of the Picts and the Scots. In the cathedral are the remains of Robert II (1371–1390), bastard son of the Wolf of Badenoch. Below the town are Birnam Woods, made famous by Shakespeare in *Macbeth*. A little further downstream is Glendelvine, where Miss Ballantine caught her 64 lb salmon in 1922.

Dunkeld has been one area to benefit from better sea-trout runs with the lessening of downstream netting. Stanley, too has seen its best sea-trout catches for years, with the average weight 4 lb in 1989.

On from Glendelvine, the Tay passes through Delvine, Kercock and Meikleour to meet the Isla on Islamouth. The Isla is a slow, unexciting river, it takes salmon up to its tributary Ericht, with its good spawning grounds and nursery beds.

At Meikleour, just above Islamouth, the Tower of Lethendy fishings have recently been timeshared on a 99-year-lease. The highest price weeks cost £350,000. At least this shows that people still have faith in the Tay.

can almost hold hands across it. One spot is
known as MacGregor's Leap, after Alexander
fishing is in February at £115 a day for five rods.
Asking prices for timeshare beats, on a 99-year-
lease, range from £10,000 a week in mid-June to
£320,000 for an October week.

One obstacle to running salmon on the lower
river is the Linn of Campsie, near Stanley where
the Tay thunders through a rocky gorge. It's a
wonderful place to watch salmon fighting their
way upstream.

Below Islamouth are the Lower Tay fishings,
with their famous beats; Almondmouth, where
the Almond comes in, Regorton, Scone, Cargill
and Taymount . . . Some fishermen would sell
their souls for a week's fishing here in autumn . . .

Notable catches on the Tay Waters, 1989

WEIGHT	ANGLER	LOCATION
31 lb	Michael Steward	Tummel
28 lb 8 oz	George Garthshore	Loch Tay
26 lb	Lindsay Bell	Dochart
26 lb	Bill Hill	Loch Tay
23 lb 8 oz	Derek Thomson	Tummel
22 lb	Mr Janetta	Loch Tay
21 lb	Duncan Twigg	Dochart
20 lb 8 oz	Mr D Glass	Loch Tay
20 lb 8 oz	Mr Gunderson	Loch Tay
20 lb	Mr Temple	Dochart
20 lb	Bob Smith	Loch Tay
19 lb 8 oz	Mr Downie	Dochart
19 lb	Ron Duncan	Tummel
18 lb	John Robertson	Lyon
18 lb	Gregor McAulay	Loch Tay
17 lb 8 oz	Maurice Williams	Tummel
17 lb	Mrs Towser	Garry
14 lb	John Clark	Lyon

LOCH TAY. Mirror
calm in the hour
before dusk. Not a
breath of wind caresses
the surface. Beautiful to
see but bad news for the
fisherman who surveys
this scene from a fishy
point of view.

7. Ross-Shire

Loch Sionascaig, Rubha Mor Lochs and The Garvie

LOCATION: Ordnance Survey Land Ranger Series, 1:50,000. Sheet 15, Loch Assynt.

GRID REFERENCES: Loch Sionascaig, 122133; Loch Buine Mor, 098154; Rubha Mor Pennisula, 990145; Irver Garvie, 039134; Loch Oscaig, 043122.

SEASONS: Salmon – April 1–October 15. Best late in season. Trout – April 1–September 30. Best, May and June.

FLIES: Salmon – Munro Killer, Garry Dog. Trout – Silver Grey, Peter Ross, Black Midge, Sedge Pupa, Black Pennell, Invicta, Grenwell's Glory, Dunkeld, Blae and Black.

COSTS: The Garvie will cost £5–£10 per rod a day; Oscaig, including boat, £15–£20 per day; and trout fishing in the area, from 75p–£5 per day.

PERMISSION: Garvie, Loch Oscaig, Loch Sionascaig and Hill Lochs: Inverpolly Estate Office, Inverpolly, Ullapool, Wester Ross (Tel: 05714–252).
Rubha More Lochs: Mrs T Longstaff, Badentarbat Lodge, Achiltibuie, Ullapool, Wester Ross (Tel: 085482–225).
Loch Lurgainn: Royal Hotel, Ullapool, Wester Ross (Tel: 0854–2181).

BEAUTIFUL WESTER ROSS is home to some of Scotland's finest fishing. Its soaring mountains, snow-capped or ablaze with heather according to the time of season, dominate every horizon. Below them, sparkling lochs and lochans are home to wild brown trout, and the cascading rivers and burns the goal of returning salmon and sea-trout.

One of the most tempting lochs in Sionascaig, in the heart of Inverpolly Nature Reserve. A first view of it steals your breath. Its waters are scattered with islands, sanctuary for birds and forbidden to anglers. Its bays teem with 8–10 oz brown trout, and a day's fishing should yield baskets up to 10 fish in the prime months, May and June. Further out, the loch plunges to more than 200 ft, its waters hiding ferox trout of up to 17 lb. Trolling is the best way to catch them, especially around the largest island, Eilean Mor.

Anglers here may have an occasional sea-eagle as company, silhouetted against the heights of surrounding Cul Beag (769 m), Cul Mor (849 m), Stac Pollaidh (612 m) and Suilven (731 m) as it swoops and turns on the air currents.

The area has a wealth of other lochs worthy of attention. The Inveppolly Estate Office is where to ask about them. Make sure you include Loch Doire na h-Airbhe, Loch Buine Moire and the Rubha Mor Lochs.

The Rubha Mor Lochs lie to the west, on the Rubha More pennisula. Most of them involve a good, stiff walk, but the reward is a day alone, broken only by the sound of lapping, sun-warmed water, or perhaps of the white Atlantic waves if you break off for a stroll along the sands.

The Garvie and Loch Oscaig can provide exciting sport with salmon and sea-trout. They, too, lie in Inverpolly Nature Reserve. The Garvie broadens into a lochan, and here and in the estuary are best places to go after sea-trout. It is harder to catch them in estuary waters as their mouths are still soft from feeding at sea. For every one you land, at least four will get away. It's frustrating, but fun.

The Garvie drains Loch Oscaig, itself good for sea-trout and brown trout, and, to the surprise of some unsuspecting anglers, the occasional salmon.

From Loch Oscaig, a single-track road weaves its way past Loch Bad a' Ghaill, Loch Lurgainn and Lochanan Dubha. All three hold brown trout of 8–12 oz and are worth fishing. Lurgainn occasionally yields a ferox trout. The bays and around the islands are the best places to fish.

LOCH SIONASCAIG. Lying in the heart of Inverpolly Nature Reserve this loch is teeming with wild brown trout. Nowhere in Scotland is the scenery as spectacular or the wildlife so abundant. Look out for sea eagles.

The Ullapool River, Gruinard and Little Gruinard

LOCATION: Ordnance Survey Land Ranger Series, 1:50,000. Sheets 20, Beinn Dearg, and 19, Gairloch and Ullapool.

GRID REFERENCES: Sheet 20, Loch Archall, 175952; **Sheet 19**, Ullapool, 125943; Gruinard Bay, 940920.

SEASONS: Salmon – May 1–September 20, with July to the end of the season the best time. Trout – April 1–September 30, with the best fishing during summer.

FLIES: Salmon – Garry Dog, Hairy Mary, Silver Stoat, Munro Killer. Trout – Invicta, various Butchers, and Blue and Black Zulus.

COSTS: For a day's sea-trout and brown-trout fishing, expect to pay £4–£15 on Ullapool. Information about the Gruinard and Little Gruinard can be obtained from the Ross and Cromarty Tourist Board, North Kessock Information Centre, Kessock, Inverness (Tel: 046373-505).

PERMISSION: Ullapool River: Loch Broom Hardware Shop, Ullapool, Ross-shire (Tel: 0854–2356).
Loch Achall: Anchor Centre, Arygle Street, Ullapool, Ross-shire (Tel: 0854–2488).
Loch Fionn: Creag Mor Hotel, Gairloch, Ross-shire (Tel: 0445–2068).

LOCH BAD a Ghaill. Waters stretch out before you like a silver carpet. To the west lie the Summer Isles, a paradise waiting to be discovered. A day fishing shallower margins will yield baskets of up to three trout.

THE FISHING VILLAGE of Ullapool gives its name to the river that hurries through it. The stream begins life in the burns draining peaty waters from rocky Seana Bhraigh (926 m) and Eidich nan Clach Geala (926 m). These burns come together as the Douchary, which tumbles down the glen over a stone and gravel bed through dark conifer plantations into Loch Achall.

The Ullapool river proper flows from this peaty loch, three miles to Loch Broom. In spate, its waters cascade through rocky gorges, rampaging over boulder-strewn rapids and swirling into deep pots and peat-stained pools. The river is split into three beats, with the best salmon fishing on the middle waters during July and August. The salmon average about 6 lb.

Sea-trout averaging nearly 2 lb can be taken on any of the beats, including Loch Achall and the estuary. The best sea-trout angling is in July and August. Loch Achall also holds small but plentiful brown trout. Fishing is boat only.

DELIGHTFUL SISTERS

Leaving Ullapool, the road heads south along the edge of Loch Broom, with the rugged summit of Beinn Dearg (1,081 m), its slopes awash with golden sedges and purple heather among the rock and scree.

The A382 coastal road finally takes us to Gruinard Bay, with, in the east, the dominating heights of An Teallach (1,062 m). This is one of Scotland's finest mountains, formed from Torridonian sandstone and shimmering with later metamorphic Cambrian quartzites.

Two delightful salmon rivers flow into Gruinard Bay. First, the Gruinard spills over its estuary sands, a 'dream' river of rocky pools and

BOTH THE Gruinard River and the Little Gruinard River splash into beautiful Gruinard Bay. Here the sea-trout gather in shoals before swimming up their native river. The mighty slopes of An Teallach (1062 m) can be seen in the background.

cascading rapids draining Loch na Sealga. It is excellent for sea-trout, which enter in July and keep coming until September, but it's salmon runs are not as prolific. Nevertheless, sport with them can be just as fast and furious. Exciting brown-trout fishing can be had on Loch na Sealga, with the fish fighting like demons. And on the loch, be prepared: a gentle tug could be the start of a fight with a 9 lb salmon.

Next to the Gruinard is the Little Gruinard, matching its big sister in spate and speed. Its salmon average about 6 lb and more than 100 are caught each year. The Boat pool is one of the best places.

The Little Gruinard drains sprawling Loch Fionn, where sea-trout, salmon and brown trout can be caught. The loch was much fished by Osgood MacKenzie, who, taking 'time-out' from laying Inverewe Gardens, would come here to seek solitude and inspiration.

Surrounding Fionn Loch are Beinn a' Chaisgein Beag (679 m), Beinn a' Chaisgen Mor (854 m), Beinn Lair (859 m) and Beinn Airigh Charr (790 m), and its waters are wave-tossed by the unrelenting winds which sweep down from the peaks. The reward for a hard day's rowing, may be a basket of 8–12 oz trout a sore back – and perhaps one of the ferox which run to more than 3 lb. Many other lochs in this areas are also well worth a visit.

The Ewe and Loch Maree

LOCATION: Ordnance Survey Land Ranger Series, 1:50,000. Sheets 19, Gairloch and Ullapool.

GRID REFERENCES: Loch Maree, 905740; Kinlochewe River, 025637; Poolewe, 856808.

SEASONS: Salmon and trout – May 1–October 31, with the best time from July onwards.

FLIES: Trout – Peter Ross, Silver Butcher, Black Pennell, Blue Zulu, Cinnamon and Gold, Teal and Silver, Dunkeld. Salmon – Garry Dog, Munro Killer, Stoat's Tail, Blue Charm.

COSTS: Some weeks of each year have been timeshared by Loch Maree Hotel. A week for 21 years will cost from £3,500–£4,500. It is worth enquiring about other weeks and days.

PERMISSION: Loch Maree: Loch Maree Hotel Achnasheen, Ross-shire (Tel: 044584–220).
Loch Maree: Kinlochewe Hotel, Kinlochewe, Ross-shire (Tel: 044584–253).
Loch Maree: P MacDonald, Kinlochewe, Ross-shire (Tel: 044584–256).
Kinlochwew River: Kinlochewe Estate Office, Kinlochewe, Ross-shire.

LOCH MAREE, OVER the mountains from Fionn Loch's southern shore, is one of Scotland's most famous sea-trout waters. It is a beautiful water, cutting a deep silver scar across Wester Ross, its many islands graced with Scot's pine, holly and ancient oak. It has a wealth of seductive bays, but in open waters plunges to depths of 300 ft and more. Most years, more than 1,000 sea-trout are taken, most of them 1–2 lb, but with many better fish among them.

Towering over Maree are Ben Slioch (980 m), the spear mountain, and Beinn Eighe (1010 m), whose lochans and burns help feed the loch. Beinn Eighe is a Nature Reserve, with trails through remnants of the ancient Caledonian forest and over purple heather and peaty moorlands, bejewelled with dark lochans. The views are stunning.

Loch Maree is split into 10 beats. Some of the best are Ash Island, Hotel Beat, Back of Island, North Shore and Gurdie. One of the biggest sea-trout taken from Maree came in 1935 and weighed 21 lb, equal to Rev A H Upcher's record sea-trout from the Awe in 1908. Dapping is the favoured method.

Sea-trout enter Maree from early season onwards, with the best runs in July and August. This is when heavier specimens arrive. Ash Island Beat gave Judge Colson a 7 lb fish in July, 1987, and North Shore a six-pounder to Mr Callander in August, 1988.

Salmon enter from the beginning of the season, but the trend in recent years has been for later runs, with more salmon being taken in the autumn.

Brown trout can provide fast-and-furious sport – but only if the sea-trout are dour.

Grey seals in Loch Ewe and even in the river are sometimes a problem, but potentially more dangerous to Maree's salmon stocks are the escapee farm salmon which are appearing. Sea-trout stocks have been boosted by the introduction in 1988 of 100,000 fry into feeder burns on the Loch Maree Estate.

A SWEET MILE

All sea-trout and salmon caught from Maree have to run the River Ewe. It is only a mile long, but offers excellent sport. Wire Pool, Tee Pool, Sea Pool and Macordies are famous pools. Fly-only is the rule and the fish run at 6–7 lb, with the usual heavier specimens.

It's worth taking a day off from fishing to visit the tropical gardens of Inverewe, started in 1862 by Osgood MacKenzie. Earth was brought in creels to cover the hard, red Torridonian sandstone and black, acid peat before anything was planted. The gardens are sheltered from winds behind a 'wooden wall' of mountain ash, Douglas fir and larch. Care of the gardens is now in the hands of the National Trust for Scotland.

LOCH MAREE. One of Scotland's most famous sea-trout waters. Up until 1678 AD, every year on the feast day of St Malrubis, patron saint of the district, a black bull was sacrificed on the little island of Innis Maree.

Shieldaig Fishings

LOCATION: Ordnance Survey Land Ranger Series, 1:50,000. Sheet 19, Gairloch and Ullapool.

GRID REFERENCES: Shieldaig Lodge, 808725.

SEASONS: Brown trout – April 1–September 30.

FLIES: Brown trout – Kingfisher Butcher, Blue Charm, Dunkeld, Silver Butcher, Peter Ross, Blue Zulu, Invicta, Greenwell's Glory, Grouse and Green, Blae and Black.

COSTS: Expect to pay up to £10 per day per rod and £250 per week for accommodation at the Lodge.

PERMISSION: Shieldaig Lodge Hotel, Badachro, Gairloch, Ross-shire (Tel: 044583–250).

SHIELDAIG, REACHED BY following the A832 from Poolewe village, at the western end of the Loch Maree, south to Gairloch, is a perfect place for a trout-fishing holiday. Literally hundred of lochs and lochans are scattered over the rugged landscape, most of them teeming with brown trout. Shieldaig Lodge Hotel is an excellent base.

The problem is where to start, but do include Fairy Loch, Lochan Sgeireach, Spectacles Loch, Diamond Loch and Loch Bad na h-Achlaise on the list. Guests at the hotel have priority over casual visitors.

Fairy Loch is hard work, but the chance of a trout of more than 2 lb makes effort worth while. Both bank and boat fishing are allowed. Lochan Sgeireach is another 'fairy loch', its waters teeming with trout of 12 oz. Fishing is from the bank only, but that is sufficient.

Spectacles Loch is set amid high, wild and desolate scenery, but it is easy to reach. Trout average 12 oz and are plentiful. Sparkling Diamond Loch also holds trout of 12 oz, with some bigger. Expect to catch a few.

Those who enjoy a good, stiff walk to their fishing, should head for Loch a' Bhealaich. Among its many trout of 12 oz are occasional specimens of 3 lb. All fight like demons.

This area of Wester Ross offers the brown trout fisher all he has ever dreamed about. The best time is in late spring and early summer, and with the right weather, and a little luck, you'll have the fishing holiday of your life.

The Alness

LOCATION: Ordnance Survey Land Ranger Series, 1:50,000. Sheet 21, Dornoch Firth.

GRID REFERENCES: Sheet 21, Loch Morie, 540755; Black Water and Alness confluence, 592746; Alness Town, 655696.

SEASONS: Salmon – February 11–October 31, with the best runs in autumn. Trout – April 1–September 30.

FLIES: Salmon – Garry Dog, Munro Killer, General Practitioner, Hairy Mary, Jeannie, Stoat's Tail. Trout – Teal and Silver, Cinnamon and Gold, Peter Ross, Black Pennell, Kingfisher Butcher, Grouse and Claret.

COSTS: A day's salmon fishing will cost around £15 per rod depending on the time of season.

PERMISSION: Alness: Novar Estates, Evanton, Ross-shire (Tel: 0349–830208).
Alness: Coul House Hotel, Contin, by Strathpeffer, Ross-shire (Tel: 0997–21487).
Alness: Patterson's, Ironmongers, High Street, Alness, Ross-shire (Tel: 0349–882286).

THE ALNESS IS far away from the trust lochs of Shieldaig, in Easter Ross, and flowing to the Cromarty Firth and the North Sea. Its waters are gathered from the desolate slopes of Carn Chuinneag (838 m), Beinn nan Eun (750 m), Meall Mor (738 m), Beinn Tharsuinn (692 m) and Meall Bhenneit (532 m), which come together in Loch Morie. A dam here means that the flow can be controlled before the river flows on to meet its main tributary, the Blackwater, the main spawning ground, at the foot of Cnoc na Stronie (310 m).

Much of Alness and Blackwater banks are suffocated by conifer plantations, which have led to flash floods and the washing away of spawning grounds. Despite this, more than 500 salmon and 300 sea-trout are taken each year, the salmon averaging 8 lb and the sea-trout $1\frac{1}{2}$ lb. Good sport can be expected (not least in the new pools and lies created by recent improvement work) from July until October, with heavier fish moving upstream from September.

The Conon and Blackwater

LOCATION: Ordnance Survey Land Ranger Series, 1:50,000. Sheets 25, Glen Carron, and 26, Inverness.

GRID REFERENCES: Sheet 25, Loch Beannacharain, 232515. **Sheet 26**, Loch Meig, 355555; Loch Luichart, 382597; Loch Achonachie, 435549; Blackwater and Conon confluence, 477548; Brahan Castle 512546.

SEASONS: Salmon – January 26–September 30, with August and September the best months. Trout – April 1–September 30, with best sport in May and June.

FLIES: Salmon – Garry Dog, Stoat's Tail, Hairy Mary, Collie Dog, Rogie, Tosh. Trout – Peter Ross, Dunkeld, Black Pennell, Blue Zulu, Silver Butcher.

COSTS: A day's fishing on Conon will cost up to £35, depending on time of season.

PERMISSION: Upper beat: J MacMillan, Newsagent, The Square, Strathpeffer, Ross-shire (Tel: 0997-21346).
Middle beat: Smiths Gore, The Square, Fochabers, Morayshire (Tel: 0463-224243).
Coul and Brahan beats: Seaforth Island Estate, Brahan, Dingwall, Ross-shire.
Contin: Coul Lodge Hotel, Contin, by Strathpeffer, Ross-shire (Tel: 0997-21487).
Strathpeffer: Craigdarroch Lodge Hotel, Contin, by Strathpeffer, Ross-shire (Tel: 0997-21265).
Strathpeffer: East Lodge Hotel: Strath Conon, Ross-shire. (Tel: 0997-222).
Lower beat: Finlayson Hughes, 45 Church Street, Inverness (Tel: 0463-224243).

SOUTH FROM THE Alness, through the townships of Dingwall and Maryburgh, the road crosses the delightful River Conon at Conon Bridge. The river draws its water from mountain burns deep in Ross-shire, amid a wilderness of heathery slopes and craggy summits.

The river has long been harnessed for hydro-electricity, with dams not only on the main rivers, but on tributaries and lochs, and with the resultant fluctuations in water-level. Two salmon counters, one at Tor Achilty Dam and one at Meig Dam, record an average of 1,300 fish and 460 fish respectively each year.

The Conon is born nearer the west coast than the east, first as Meig flowing into Loch Beannacharain below the summits of Bac an Eich (849 m). A torrential stream here, it keeps the name Meig as it hurries from the loch to gather in more feeder burns before finally widening into Loch Meig in Strathconon.

The Conon proper begins at the outlet from the loch and is soon met, at Little Scatwell, by the outflow from Loch Luichart.

The swollen Conon flows on down the strath, between pastures and trees, into Loch Achonachie, at the edge of Torrachilty Forest. From here to the estuary, its course is meandering and lazy but still to be joined by the Blackwater, at Little Moy, and the river Orrin, which flows in under the auspicious eye of the ruins of Brahan Castle.

The upper Conon was bought from the Hydro Board a few years ago by Loch Achonachie Angling Club for £70,000, and the club also purchased the tributary Blackwater. Lower Conon beats have been timeshared in the prime months and are then difficult of access, though they are available at other times. The Cromarty District Council has the rights to the estuary fishing.

LEGENDARY TROUT

Upper Conon fishings are best in September and October. In 1989, 139 salmon were taken. The Blackwater, fishings, from the mouth of Loch na Croic to just below the Falls of Rogie, gave 80 fish in 1987.

The Brahan beats usually fish extremely well. In July, 1988, during a superb run of grilse and salmon, three weeks saw 447 fish caught. In those same weeks, 311 fish were taken from the Blackwater. And that same season saw no fewer than 1,500 sea-trout caught from the estuary in July and August.

Brown-trout fishing is also excellent throughout the Conon system. It was from Loch Garve, at the head of the Blackwater, that one angler took a 26 lb trout in September, 1892. I wonder if monster trout are like the Phoenix and appear only once every 100 years. Guess where I'll be on September 17 1992, just in case . . .

8. Lomond and Argyll

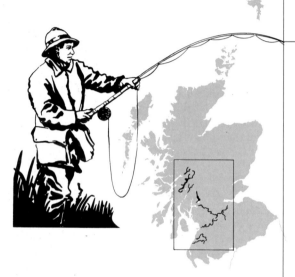

The Clyde

LOCATION: Ordnance Survey Land Ranger Series, 1:50,000. Sheets 78, Nithsdale and Lowther Hills; 72, Upper Clyde Valley; 64, Glasgow.

GRID REFERENCES: Sheet 72, Roberton, 945285; Lamington, 978313; Thankerton, 974383; Carstairs Junction, 953455; Lanark, 880438; Kirkfield, 862436; Crosford, 826467.

SEASONS: Trout – March 15–September 30, with the best sport in early summer and August.

FLIES: Trout – Black Spider, Greenwell's Glory, Iron Blue Dun, Blae and Black.

COSTS: An annual ticket will cost around £12, with day tickets available at £2.

PERMISSION: Roberton to Thankerton: Lamington and District Angling Association, Secretary, B F Dexter, 18 Boghall Park, Biggar, Lanarkshire.
Roberton, Carstairs, Crawford, Lanark and Motherwell: United Clyde Angling Protective Association, Secretary, J Quigley, 39 Hillfoot Avenue, Wishaw, Lanarkshire, ML2 8TR.
Lanark: Lanark and District Angling Association, W Frood, 82 Rhyber Avenue, Lanark (please enclose SAE).
   Most fishing-tackle shops in Glasgow issue permits.

THE CLYDE IS a river of the future. Gone forever are the days of heavy industrial activity. Excellent work by the Clyde River Purification Board has led to the cleaning and restocking of the river, the creation and improvement of pools and lies, and the buying-out of estuary nets. And at last the river has seen the return of salmon and sea-trout.

The Clyde's source is amid the Lowther Hills, just a couple of miles from Wells of Tweed. Its waters tumble northwards, stealing hundreds of frothy burns from rounded, windswept hills. These upper reaches are delightful brown-trout waters, with fish of 8–12 oz trout.

But as the river increases in size, so do its trout, and the best places for brown-trout fishing are on lower reaches. Crossford, Hazelbank, Kirkfield and Crawford all yielded trout of more than 2 lb in 1989; and at Carstairs Junction, John Gauld landed a brown trout of 2 lb 8 oz that same year.

Anglers now have the bonus of occasional sea-trout and salmon, although fishing for migratory fish is restricted at present. But perhaps future generations will once more know the thrill of landing salmon of more than 40 lb and sea-trout topping 14 lb, as anglers on this river once did.

L OCH LOMMOND. As well as brown trout the loch holds salmon and sea-trout. Try fishing round the islands for best results. The waters are also used for water sports and anglers should bare this in mind when planning their assault.

The Ayr, The Water of Girvan and The Stinchar

THE AYR

LOCATION: Ordnance Survey Land Ranger Series, 1:50,000. Sheets 71, Lanark and Upper Nithsdale, and 70, Ayr and Kilmarnock.

GRID REFERENCES: Sheet 71, Glenbuck Loch, 756286; Achinleck, 555225; **Sheet 70**, Catrine Weir, 536262; Mauchline, 502273; Ayr, 338223.

SEASONS: Salmon – February 11–October 31, with autumn the best time. Trout – March 15–September 30, with the summer producing most fish.

FLIES: Salmon – General Practitioner, Thunder and Lightning, Garry Dog, Munro Killer, Stoat's Tail. Trout – Peter Ross, Grouse and Claret, March Brown, Teal and Silver.

COSTS: A day's fishing on Ayr will cost only about £2 – excellent value for money.

PERMISSION: Auchinleck: Auchinleck Angling Association, J McColm, 21 Milne Avenue, Auchinleck, Ayrshire.
Mauchline: Mauchline, Ballochymylke Angling Club, J F McCall, Post Office, High Street Mauchline, Ayrshire.
Ayr: Director of Finance, Kyle and Carrick District Council, Town Buildings, Ayr (Tel: 0292–269141).
Ayr: James Kirk, Union Arcade, Burns Statue Square, Ayr.

THE WATER OF GIRVAN

LOCATION: Ordnance Survey Land Ranger Series, 1:50,000. Sheets 77, New Galloway and Glen Trool, and 76, Girvan.

GRID REFERENCES: Sheet 77, Loch Bradan Reservoir, 423973; Blairquhan, 367056. **Sheet 76**, Crosshill, 325066, Bargany, 243003; Girvan, 187982.

SEASONS: Salmon – February 25–October 31, with best runs in autumn. Trout – March 15–October 6, with best sport in May, June and August.

FLIES: Salmon – Stoat's Tail, Executioner, Thunder and Lightning, Silver Stoat. Trout – Peter Ross, Cinnamon and Gold, Black Pennell, March Brown.

COSTS: A day's salmon fishing on Ayr will cost about £8.

PERMISSION: Blairquhan Estate: Gamekeeper, Blairquhan Estate, Straiton, Ayrshire (Tel: 046588–272).
Kilkerran Estate: Gamekeeper, Kilkerran Estate, Crosshill, Ayrshire (Tel: 06554–278).
Bargany Estate: Gamekeeper, Bargany Estate, Dailly, Ayrshire (Tel: 046581–437).
Girvan: Carrick Angling Club, J Murray, Tackle-dealer, Dalrymple Street, Girvan, Ayrshire.

THE STINCHAR

LOCATION: Ordnance Survey Land Ranger Series, 1:50,000. Sheets 77, New Galloway and Glen Trool, and 76, Girvan.

GRID REFERENCES: Sheet 77, Cairnadloch Hill, 395941. **Sheet 76**, Barr 275940; Dalreoch Water, 163864; Colmonell Water, 150856; Knockdolian Water, 125855; Kirkholm Water, 112838.

SEASONS: Salmon – February 25–October 31, with most fish caught in autumn. Trout – March 15–October 6, with best sport in summer.

FLIES: almon – Stinchar Stoat's Tail, Silver Stoat, Blue Charm, Thunder and Lightning, General Practitioner. Trout – Peter Ross, March Brown, Silver Butcher, Grouse and Claret, Black Spider.

COSTS: A day's salmon fishing on Stinchar in prime autumn weeks will cost £40 per rod.

PERMISSION: Ballantrae: Mr R Dalrymple, Crailoch Farm, Ballantrae (Tel: 046583–418).
Kirkholm: Mr and Mrs Marshal, Kirkholm Farm, Ballantrae, Ayrshire (Tel: 046583–297).
Knockdolian Estate: Knockdolian Estate Office, Alderside, Colmonell, Girvan, Ayrshire (Tel: 046588–237).
Bardrochat Estate: R Anderson, Oaknowe, Bardrochat Estate, Colmonell, Ayrshire (Tel: 046588–202).
Dalreoch Estate: D Overend, Dalreoch Estate Office, Colmonell, Ayrshire.
Boar's Head Water: Boar's Head Hotel, Colmonell, Ayrshire (Tel: 046588–272).

RIVER STINCHER. Around Pinwherry the river is hemmed in by trees making casting difficult. Do persevere as this gentle little river is home not only to beautiful brown trout but some surprisingly large salmon as well.

THE AYR, WATER of Girvan and Stinchar lie south from the Clyde, and all flow from each to west.

The Ayr is wide and shallow, and flooding is not uncommon on its lower reaches. Its salmon and sea-trout run from early August, with salmon averaging about 6 lb and sea-trout $1\frac{1}{2}$ lb.

The Ayr begins its journey from Glenbuck Loch, sheltered by rounded Hareshaw Hill (465 m). It gathers in many feeder burns, from here to the Firth of Clyde, draining most of Ayrshire. Its chattering course is over gravel and round stony islands, its banks graced with hazel, alder, willow, oak and beech through Ayrshire's buttercup meadows.

The best salmon and sea-trout fishing on the Ayr is from the weir at Catrine to the estuary, and as netting rights are bought-out, and poachers caught, it should get even better. The river's brown trout offer excellent sport and run at 8–12 oz. The river is stocked each year.

South of Ayr, the A77 road reaches Girvan town, beside the estuary of the Water of Girvan, flowing from Little Loch Girvan Eye high on Craigmasheenie (539 m). The young river tumbles from the loch's northern end through dense Tairlaw Plantation and passes through three more lochs on its seaward journey. Its flow from the third loch, Loch Bradan Reservoir, is restricted by Bradan Dam.

Girvan's upper reaches are inaccessible to salmon because of the insurmountable falls of Tranew Linn and are 'trout only' waters. But with no netting, a fish hatchery, and an active Improvement Association, the river is one to be noted. Its fishing represents excellent value for money.

But of all the Ayrshire rivers, the best is without doubt the Stinchar. Its clear tumbling burns rush down from Cairnadloch (475 m) and surrounding hills to join and splash over a series of falls before flowing more quietly over gravel and through pools. The Duisk and water of Tig are the main tributaries. The main river has some excellent lies and pools.

Salmon and sea-trout spawn throughout the length of the river and in its tributaries. No stocking is done and there is a limited amount of estuary netting. Despite this, several hundred salmon and sea-trout are caught each season. Recent seasons have seen the appearance of rainbow trout, fish-farm escapees which have come down the Firth of Clyde. Fish of more than 3 lb have been caught.

Some of the best salmon fishing on Stinchar is on the Duke of Wellington's Knockdolian Estate. Each season sees around 460 salmon and 300 sea-trout caught, with the salmon taken mostly during autumn, and the sea-trout in July and August. Average weights are 8 lb for salmon and about 1½ lb for sea-trout. The excellence of the Knockdolian beats is reflected in the price. At prime times a day's fishing will cost £40.

Some Stinchar beats are totally private and elsewhere fishing can be difficult to obtain. Advance booking is essential – and do a rain-dance before you go. Stinchar headwaters are tapped by man and the river is dependant on good rainfall to keep it fishable.

The Awe, Loch Awe and Orchy

LOCATION: Ordnance Survey Land Ranger Series, 1:50,000. Sheets 50, Glen Orchy, and 55, Lochgilphead.

GRID REFERENCES: Sheet 50, Loch Awe, 090235; Pass of Brander, 055277; Taynuilt, 005311; Dalmally, 161271; Orchy and Lochy confluence, 192277; Lochan na Bi, 307315; Loch Tulla, 300430; Bridge of Orchy, 299396. **Sheet 55,** Loch Awe 945075.

SEASONS: Salmon – February 15–October 15, with best fishing in autumn. Trout – March 15–October 6, with fishing best in May, June, July and August.

FLIES: Salmon – Stoat's Tail, Garry Dog, Executioner, General Practitioner, Thunder and Lightning, Silver Stoat. Trout – Black Pennell, Peter Ross, Greenwell's Glory, Grouse and Claret, Dunkeld, Ke-He.

COSTS: A week's timeshare on Craig fishings on Orchy will cost up to £69,000 in perpetuity. Other Orchy fishing is available from £7 per rod per day. Fishing on Loch Awe is free, but a day on the River Awe will cost up to £40.

PERMISSION: Awe: Inverawe and Taynuilt Fisheries, Argyll (Tel: 08662–262).
Orchy: Savills, 12 Clerk Street, Brechin, Angus (Tel: 03562–2187).
Orchy: W A Church, Croggan Crafts, Dalmally, Argyll (Tel: 08382–201).
Orchy and Loch Awe: Carraig Thura Hotel, Lochawe Village, by Dalmally, Argyll (Tel: 08382–210).
Loch Awe: Dalmally Hotel, Dalmally, Argyll (Tel: 08382–444)

Loch Awe: Ardbrecknish House, by Dalmally, Argyll (Tel: 08663–223).
Loch Awe: Portsonachan Hotel, Kilchrenan, by Dalmally, Argyll (Tel: 08663–224).
Loch Awe: Taychreggan Hotel, Kilchrenan, by Dalmally, Argyll (Tel: 08663–211).
Loch Awe: Ford Hotel, Ford, Argyll (Tel: 054681–273).
Loch Awe: Ardanàiseig Hotel, Kilchrenan, by Taynuilt, Argyll (Tel: 08663–333).
Many other lochs in the area are worthy of attention. Oban and Lorn Angling Club will advise.
Hill Lochs: Oban and Lorn Angling Club, David Graham, 9–15 Crombie Street, Oban, Argyll (Tel: 0631–62029).

THE AWE DRAINS one of Scotland's most spectacular waters, Loch Awe. It is split into seven highly desirable and expensive beats, all hard to come by. If you do manage a day, then you may catch a fish for the glass-case. A fly-only river, Awe tumbles down the historic Pass of Brander to discharge into salt water in Loch Etive.

This dark, inhospitable pass is where King Robert Bruce of Scotland had his revenge over the Clan MacDougall in 1308. He was determined to break their hold on power in Argyll, and massed his troops around the pass, some warriors rolling

LOCH AWE. No fishing career is complete without a visit here. Although it is crowded at the northern end southern bays offer solitude from fellow anglers, but fortunately, not the trout which are in plentiful supply.

RIVER ORCHY. A crisp autumn morning and the river still low from summer, flows gently to mingle with the waters of mighty Loch Awe. Prime weeks on Craig Beat of Orchy have been time shared. Four rods fishing in perpetuity will cost £69,000.

huge boulders down the sides. It was a notable victory for Bruce. Fleeing MacDougalls were carried away by the torrential waters of Awe, and it is said that the river ran red.

Its waters are now harnessed for hydro-electricity and the flow through the dam is regulated, so that the river downstream is but a shadow of its former self. Despite this, more than 3,300 fish are counted through the barrage each season. UDN, present in the river for the past 20 years, is gradually declining, though disease-marked fish are still taken.

WOODED BANKS AND FORESTRY FLOODING

The Awe is famous for the size of its salmon. In 1921 Major Huntingdon had one of 57 lb. Two years later, Mr Thornton took two-and-a-half hours to land a 56-pounder. In 1927 Mrs Huntingdon caught a 55 lb salmon, and in 1930 had another of 51 lb. Good runs of salmon come in from July onwards, but the big fish enter the river mainly in autumn. Sea-trout are also caught, the biggest taken by Rev Upcher from Bothie Pool in 1908. It weighed 21 lb. The best months for sea-trout are late June and July.

Flowing from Pass of Brander, the lower reaches of the river are through fertile meadows banked by silver birch, oak and beech.

Loch Awe is shaped like a trout, with the Awe and the Orchy forming the tail. Most Awe salmon spawn grounds in the Orchy, a beautiful, tumbling water flowing from Loch Tulla down steep Glen Orchy. It was in this glen that the poet Duncan Ban MacIntyre was born in the 1700s.

On its way down the glen the Orchy gathers in the Lochy, which flows down Glen Lochy from Lochan na Bi, its banks heavily planted with conifers. Then, just before the Orchy spills into Loch Awe, it is met by its tributary Strae. Unfortunately, flash floods are the result of forestry work have resulted in many spawning grounds being washed away. More than 50 per cent of Argyll is down to forestry. How did we let it happen?

The best Orchy fishing is to be had on the two-mile Craig Beat, six miles downstream from Bridge of Orchy. The beat has 21 named pools and a five-year average of 90 fish. Recently it has been timeshared. For four rods to fish one week each year, in perpetuity, will cost £46,000–£69,000.

At the Orchy estuary stands Kilchurn Castle's grey ruins. It was an ancient seat of Breadalbane Campbells and was used to house Government troops during the 1745 uprising.

Towering over Loch Awe are mountains of the majestic Cruachan range. Awe is the longest inland loch in Scotland, cutting a scar more than 25 miles long through Argyll. In its southern area its waters plunge more than 270 ft, 60 ft deeper than at the northern end. Much of her banks are clad with conifers.

FROM GALLEYS TO DINGHIES

Most salmon taken from Loch Awe come from northern end, in the 'tail-fin' of the loch. Angling around the islands can produce excellent sport. One of them Fraoch Eilean, has castle ruins, once the stronghold of Lorne, defeated by Bruce I of Scotland in the Pass of Brander. He protected this castle and Kilchurn with the aid of three galley-ships. They must have made a magnificent sight. Nowadays, the boats on the loch are largely fishing dinghies.

As well as salmon, sea-trout and brown trout, Awe holds rainbow trout, perch, char and pike, which attract hundreds of anglers each season. But with a good outboard, it is still easy to find an empty bay to fish.

The best time for brown trout is in April and May. In 1866 Mr W Muir took a 39 lb 8 oz brown trout. Unfortunately, the cast of the fish was lost in a fire. Even now people argue as to whether it was a salmon or a ferox.

Recently arrived rainbow trout have caused havoc with stocks of fry and smolt. They came from a fish-farm, and now some of them are enormous. In 1986 Mr Graham took one of 21 lb 4 oz. The 1988 season saw rainbows taken of 11 lb 12 oz, 13 lb and 14 lb, and one angler had 19 rainbows for a day, five of them more than 7 lb.

Loch Awe can be a dangerous water. Winds sweeps along her length, tossing white-crested waves before it, and it is always wise to head for shelter when the skies darken and the water turns grey – and always wear a lifejacket.

The Shira, Douglas, Fyne, Aray and Eachaig

LOCATION: Ordnance Survey Land Ranger Series, 1:50,000. Sheet 56, Loch Lomond.

GRID REFERENCES: Inveraray, 096085; Glen Shira, 135145; Glen Fyne, 226157; Douglas Water, 053056; Eachaig, 141847; Loch Eck, 138915.

SEASONS: Salmon – May 1–October 15, with July and August best. Loch Eck does not close until 31st October. Trout – April 1–September 30, with best sport in early summer and August.

FLIES: Salmon – Hairy Mary, Silver Stoat, Stoat's Tail, Thunder and Lightning, Garry Dog. Trout – Black Pennell, Blue Zulu, Soldier Palmer, Bibio, Dunkeld, Invicta.

COSTS: Salmon-fishing on the Eachaig will cost £290 per rod per week. Loch Eck is available for around £20 per day for two rods and a boat with outboard motor. Expect to pay £10–£15 per rod per day on Shira, Douglas, Fyne and Aray.

PERMISSION: Shire, Douglas, Array: Factor, Argyll Estates Office, Cherry Park, Inveraray, Argyll (Tel: 0499–2203).
Douglas: Argyll Caravan Park, Inveraray, Argyll (Tel: 0499–2285).
Fyne: Ardinglas Estate Office, Inveraray, Argyll (Tel: 04996–217).
Fyne: Cairndow Estate Office, Inveraray, Argyll (Tel: 04996–284).
Eachaig and Loch Eck: Salar Properties Limited, Lochloy House, Nairn (Tel: 0667–55355).
Loch Eck: Whistlefield Inn, Loch Eck, by Dunoon, Argyll (Tel: 036986–250).
Loch Eck: Dunoon and District Angling Club, A H Young, 7 Blair Lane, Dunoon, Argyll.

OVER THE MOUNTAINS to the south of Loch Awe are four delightful rivers. The A819 road closely follows the course of one, the Aray, as it charges down Glen Aray to flow past Inveraray Castle into sea Loch Fyne. Inveraray, capital of Argyll, was made a Royal Burgh in 1648.

Netting at the river mouth considerably reduces rod-catches on the Aray, but they are still good and come mostly from the lower pools.

Entering Loch Fyne further south, on its western shores, is Douglas Water. Salmon and sea-trout are unable to run more than a couple of miles upstream because of an impassable falls. In summer, the river can become a mere trickle, but the few pools on the lower reaches can be productive of salmon in late summer and autumn. July is best for sea-trout.

Entering Loch Fyne from the north are the Shira and Fyne. Both rivers have been harnessed for hydro electricity. Salmon and sea-trout run from July.

From Strachur, on Loch Fyne's eastern shores, the A815 road runs down past Loch Eck and the river that connects it with Holy Loch, the Eachaig. With more than 40 pools, the Eachaig produces an average of 160 salmon and 500 sea-trout each season from its three rotating beats, but the best months have been timeshared. In 1989 Mr Clarkson caught a 15 lb 8 oz sea-trout while fishing a Willie Gunn on Ashtree Pool.

Most of Loch Eck is surrounded by forestry, but salmon and sea-trout fishing is still good, and best from August. The northern end, where Cur flows in, is good, and trolling produces good results anywhere. In places Loch Eck plunges to more than 120 ft deep, and no doubt, some ferox are lurking in the depths.

Loch Lomond, Leven and Endrick

LOCATION: Ordnance Survey Land Ranger Series, 1:50,000. Sheets 56, Loch Lomond, and 63, Firth of Clyde.

GRID REFERENCES: Sheet 56, Loch Lomond, 332034; Loch Lomond, 380890; Endrick Mouth, 425896. **Sheet 63**, River Leven, 390785.

SEASONS: Trout – March 15–September 30, with May, June, July and August best. Salmon – February 11–October 31, with the best sport in mid-summer.

FLIES: Trout – Peter Ross, Dunkeld, Invicta, Bibio, Soldier Palmer, Little Red Sedge, Iron Blue Dun, Blae and Black, Black Spider, Greenwell's Glory, Starling Tip, Dark Olive, Golden Olive, Mallard and Gold, Mallard and Silver. Salmon – Turkey and Gold, Blue Charm, Thunder and Lightning.

COSTS: Fishing on Loch Lomond will cost £7.50 for a day ticket and £22 weekly. The Endrick is available at around £15 per rod per day. Charges for the Leven are available on request.

BOATS: Available from MacFarlane and Sons, Balmaha, Argyll (Tel: 036087-214).

PERMISSION: Loch Lomond, Leven and Endrick: Loch Lomond Angling Improvement Association, R A Clement and Company, 29 Vincent Place, Glasgow, (Tel: 041221-0068).

LOCH LOMOND IS perhaps Scotland's most famous loch, and restocking and good management are gradually making it one of its finest fisheries. It covers 27 square miles and is more than 450 ft deep at its deepest point. Its innumerable wooded islands add to its wealth of scenery, culminating in massive Ben Lomond (974 m).

In the distant past the islands provided sanctuary to mainlanders who fled to them with their animals. It wasn't always a good idea. Norse King Haakon sailed up neighbouring Loch Long in 1263 with his warriors. They carried their gallies over land to Loch Lomond, relaunched them and laid waste the islands. Later, in the 1700s, the islands were used to house drunkards and lunatics. Nowadays, they are peaceful wildlife sanctuaries.

Loch Lomond gathers its water from the surrounding mountains, its tributaries hurrying down steep gullies on its northern shores and meandering across the flat lands on the southern side. Most important is the Endrick, draining the Gargunnock and Fintry Hills and flowing west through fertile pastures and rolling moorlands before spilling into Lomond a mile south of Balmaha.

Salmon and sea-trout enter the Endrick from July. Good pools are Coolies Linn, Meetings Linn, Oak Tree and Cowden Mill Dam. All have yielded salmon and sea-trout of more than 10 lb in recent seasons. Trolling off Endrick mouth can give good sport.

Lomond also holds a whitefish, the powan, known as the freshwater herring. During the last war these were netted as food, but they are seldom caught by anglers.

REMOTE RICHES

Brown trout are caught all along Lomond's shores, but the northern reaches are the most productive. An advantage in fishing the remoter parts of the loch is that probably you will fish alone. The trout run from 8–12 oz and are best fished for when there is a slight breeze.

Migratory fish reach Lomond through the short River Leven, which connects with the Clyde. It is a meandering, sluggish river with long, deep, gravelly pools, and it is heavily fished.

In August, 1989, 575 salmon and grilse were taken. That same month saw a catch of 1,300 sea-trout. September produced similar results. One angler ended a day's fishing with 18 sea-trout from 4 lb to 9 lb.

Lomond's salmon average about 10 lb, though bigger fish are taken regularly. Some of the best lies are around the islands – Inchtavannach, Inchmoan, Inchconnchan, Inchcruin, Inchford and Inchfad. But the visitor does well to seek local advice.

LOCH LOMOND. Most famous of all Scotlands waters. The leisure boats that grace the waters today are a far cry from those gallies of warring Norse King Haakon and his warriors in 1263. Battles of today rage only between man and fish.

9. The Royal Dee

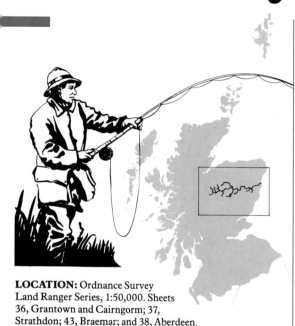

LOCATION: Ordnance Survey Land Ranger Series, 1:50,000. Sheets 36, Grantown and Cairngorm; 37, Strathdon; 43, Braemar; and 38, Aberdeen.

GRID REFERENCES: Sheet 36, Wells of Dee, 937987. **Sheet 34,** Chest of Dee, 013886; White Bridge, 019885; Linn of Dee, 062897; Mar Lodge, 096899; Braemar, 150915. **Sheet 37,** Ballater, 370955; Dinnet, 460986; Aboyne, 524983; Potarch Bridge, 607973. **Sheet 38,** Banchory, 695965; Park, 782975.

SEASONS: February 1–September 30, with March, April and September the best months.

FLIES: Blue Charm, Logie, General Practitioner, Silver Blue, Jeannie, Munro Killer, Shrimp Fly, March Brown, Gordon, Akroyd, Mar Lodge.

COSTS: Fishing prices vary, depending upon the beat and time of year. On the lower river, back-end day-lets may be obtained for £15/£20 per rod; at prime times, the cost per rod may be as much as £300/£500 per week. Preference is always given to guests who book all the rods on a beat. Day-lets are rarely available at prime times.

ACCOMMODATION: Full details of accommodation on Deeside may be obtained from Paul Higson, Area Tourist Officer, Kincardine and Deeside Tourist Board, 45 Station Road, Banchory, Aberdeenshire, AB3 3XX (Tel: Banchory 033–02–2066). Expect to pay £250/£300 for a week's full-board accommodation, including picnic lunches. At the upper end of the market (Invery House), prices are considerably more.

PERMISSION: Mar Lodge Estate: Braemar (Tel: 03383–216).
Invercauld Arms Hotel: Braemar (Tel: 03383–605).
Banchory Lodge Hotel: Banchory (Tel: 03302–2625).
J Somers, 40 Thistle Street, Aberdeen (Tel: 0224–639910).
Macsport Limited: Ballater Road, Aboyne (Tel: 0339–86896).
Macsport Limited: 27 High Street, Banchory (Tel: 03302–2855).
Scotia Sporting Services: Aboyne (Tel: 0339–2465).
Invery House: Banchory (Tel: 03302–4782).
Leys Estate: St Nicholas, 68 Station Road, Banchory (Tel: 03302–3343).
Ardoe House Hotel: Blairs, by Aberdeen (Tel: 0224–867355).
Mrs Green, Lodge Gate House, Ardoe, Kincardineshire (Tel: 0224–867752).
Bell Ingram Ltd: Durn, Isla Road, Perth (Tel: 0738–21121).
Savills: 12 Clerk Street, Brechin (Tel: 035–62–2187).
Scottish Sporting Services: Watten, Caithness (Tel: 0955–82–209).
Tullich Lodge: by Ballater, Aberdeenshire (Tel: 0338–55406).
Craigendarroch Hotel: Braemar Road, Ballater (Tel: 0338–55858).
Invercauld Estate: Estate Office, Braemar (Tel: 033–83–224).
Glentanar Estate: Estate Office, Aboyne (Tel: 0339–2451).
Mr A Campbell, Altries, Maryculter, Aberdeen, AB1 0BD.
Mrs De Winton, Hopewell, Tarland, Aberdeenshire (Tel: 03398–81239).
Ms Wendy Coy, Amber Hill, Boston, Lincolnshire (Tel: 0205–79-444).
Charleston Hotel: Aboyne (Tel: Aboyne 0339-2476).
Earl & Lawrence Prudential: Estates Division, 55 Northgate, Sleaford, Lincolnshire NG34 7AB (Tel: 0529-302946).
Birse Lodge Hotel: Aboyne (Tel: 0339-2253).
Howie Irvine: 62 Bon Accord Street, Aberdeen (Tel: 0224-580913).
Nick Carter, Kenmay, Aberdeenshire (Tel: 0467-43485).

THE MAGNIFICENT ROYAL Dee is the jewel of Scottish salmon rivers. Born amid the wild Cairngorm Mountains, it bubbles from the Wells of Dee on the slopes of Braeriach, 1,219 m above sea level, beside an ice-white, quartz cairn. From these distant pools, Dee begins its 85-mile journey to the granite city of Aberdeen and the cold, grey waters of the North Sea; thundering down the inhospitable, grit-strewn slopes of the Lairig Ghru, one of

RIVER DEE. Looking upstream from the bridge at Ballater you can see the grey slopes of the Grampian mountains climbing skywards. In Country Wear fishing tackle shop in Ballater is the cast of a 42 lb salmon caught by the most famous Dee fisherman, Arthur Wood.

Scotland's highest passes.

Allt a'choire Mhoir, Gharb Choire and Clach nan Taillear burns tumble in from Ben Macdhui (1,311 m) and Cairn Toul (1,293 m), flowing past Clach nan Taillear Stone and Corrour Bothy, guarded by the dark cliffs of the Devil's Point, gathering waters from Glen Geusachan and hurrying them through Glen Dee, past Chest of Dee, to their meeting with Allt an t-Seilich at White Bridge.

Chest of Dee is a long staircase of broken rocks and pools where the waters surge and boil in unending fury, sending an incandescent spray shimmering above the falls. After heavy rains, or when winter snow melts from the high mountains, Chest of Dee roars its defiance to the skies.

White Bridge lies at the north end of a dramatic, 12-hour walk from Blair Atholl Castle in Perthshire, by Glen Tilt, to Deeside; a journey through some of Scotland's wildest scenery, much admired by Queen Victoria and that most caustic observer of all things Scottish, the Welshman, Thomas Pennant.

A series of fine walking tracks fan out from White Bridge; south, past the ruin of Bynack Lodge to Loch Tilt; west, by the Geldie Burn and Duke's Chair to the headwaters of the Feshie; and north, into the wilderness of Cairngorm.

An open valley greets the growing river, surrounded on either side by range after range of blue hills, alive with grouse and the piping of curlew, where man has hunted and fished for thousands of years, from Neolithic times. Stags haunt the high places and these lands are one of the most productive deer-forests in Scotland.

Salmon rest lazily in the turbulent stream, exhausted by their long, dangerous passage from the sea and hard fight through the foaming torrent of Linn of Dee, a narrow, dark, chasm, and the only natural obstacle to returning fish throughout the length of the river.

However, by the time salmon reach the upper Dee, they have been in the river for several weeks, and their silver Atlantic sheen has turned to the red blaze of autumn spawning. Few fresh fish are encountered here, and salmon are best left in peace to get on with their proper business, the propagation of their species.

SALMON LEAPING

For centuries, Kings and Queens of Scotland come to Mar to hunt and stalk; Mary, Queen of Scots was entertained there, in 1563, in the valley of the Tilt, where a handsome palace was built for her comfort while she enjoyed the 'tinchal', a great deer-hunt:

> The Queen, with her numerous attendants and a great concourse of the nobility, gentry, and people, were assembled at the appointed glen, and the spectacle much delighted her Majesty . . . The Queen's stag-hounds and those of the nobility were loosed, and a successful chase ensued. Three hundred and sixty deer were killed, five wolves, and some roes.

In more recent times Britain's monarchs have journeyed north to take part in deer drives organised each year by the local laird. The drive was always held on a Saturday, when the King would drive over from Balmoral for the day.

Linn of Dee is a favourite salmon-watching spot. A narrow, tree-lined road twists west from Braemar, crossing the Linn before returning east by Claybokie and Mar. A locked gate bars vehicle access to the Upper Dee, although the tracks are open to hill-walkers.

But most visitors come to see salmon leaping the falls. Some have looked too closely, and a memorial plaque commemorates the fate of two unwary visitors who drowned in the Linn in 1927.

A path leads from the roadside to the edge of the Linn, which grips the river between black, high-sided banks extending for a distance of some 60 yards. Through this deep, narrow passage, Dee pours in majesty, and it is often possible to watch salmon lying in the dark waters, waiting for the moment when they must continue their upstream journey.

Below the Linn, Dee widens into a broad, crystal-clear stream, banked by ancient Scots pine; and the scent of pine resin and the soft feel of fallen pine needles beneath one's feet becomes fixed in the mind of all who walk and fish the upper reaches of the river.

Mar Lodge, on the north bank, has had a chequered career. The magnificent house was built by Queen Victoria in the late nineteenth century for the Duke of Fife, who married Victoria's eldest daughter, Princess Louise. The Duke and his Princess are remembered on Deeside by the park which hosts the Braemar Games, dedicated to their name.

Until 1988, Mar Lodge was owned by Swiss businessman, Gerald Panchaud, who did much to improve the old house and its sporting facilities; now, the estate has changed hands again and is the home of a wealthy American industrialist, whose plans for Mar are uncertain.

The valley of the Dee is filled with reminders

of Scotland's turbulent past; one is Braemar Castle, built in 1682 by the eighteenth Earl of Mar as a fortress against the ambitions of his warlike neighbour, Farquharson of Invery.

Braemar Castle lasted seven years before being burned by John Farquharson, the Black Colonel, who punished Mar for his failure to support the Jacobite cause. The Earl of Mar, known as 'Bobbing Johnnie', because of his frequent changes of allegiance, used to summon his servants and tenants by firing his pistol in the air.

After his fine new castle had been burned, Mar enthusiastically eschewed the Jacobite cause. In August 1715, he returned to Mar and plotted rebellion. On September 6 he raised the Jacobite standard at Invercauld and ordered his tenants to join him.

THE OLD PRETENDER

Few were willing to do so, and many had to be persuaded, such as Forbes of Inverernan. Mar wrote to Black Jock: 'Jocke, Ye was in the right not to come with the 100 men ye sent up to-night, when I expected four times the number. Particularly let my tenants in Kildrummy know, that if they come not forth with their best arms, I will send a party immediately to burn what they shall miss taking from them.'

Gentle persuasion, indeed, but to little avail. The mad adventure ended on the grim heights of Sheriffmuir, near Dunblane, when Government forces commanded by the Duke of Argyll faced Mar in indecisive battle. By February, 1716, James, The Old Pretender, and his lieutenants had fled to France; and Braemar Castle was burned to the ground again.

Invercauld is still the home of the Farquhar-

sons, and it was there, in the summer of 1881, that Robert Louis Stevenson wrote most of his famous novel, *Treasure Island*; eight miles north from Braemar stands the old Gordon House, leased by Queen Victoria as her Highland home.

The property obviously 'amused' Victoria,

because she bought it in 1848 for £100,000. The house was rebuilt and enlarged to the design of local architect, William Smith, of Aberdeen, and renamed Balmoral; the favourite retreat of two of the most famous salmon anglers in the world, The Queen Mother and her grandson, The Prince of

RIVER DEE. By the old Brig' of Dee at Invercauld. Captain Alwyne Farquharson with his head keeper, Donald MacDonald. Although other Scottish rivers have seen a decline in their spring fishing the Dee still offers anglers first class sport.

Wales.

The Dee is a royal river in every sense, and throughout its length, from the sea to the Linn, Dee offers some of the best salmon fishing in Europe. While most other major Scottish rivers have seen spring runs of salmon drastically decline in recent years, the Dee still provides outstanding sport in the early months of the season.

But it can be cold, hard work and at times, in February and March, the river is unfishable due to the jigsaw puzzle of ice-flows, known locally as 'grue', flooding downstream. However, from opening day on February 1 until the end of the season on September 30, fish run the river, with fresh salmon still being caught in autumn months.

Upstream movement of salmon is dictated by prevailing weather conditions and water levels. A hard winter in the Cairngorms is good news for the Dee. Melting snow metres out the flow and provides excellent fishing conditions well into May, when other rivers are beginning to feel the pinch of summer drought.

This vast, mountain reservoir can also be dangerous, and, over the years, cloud-bursts in the Cairngorms, combined with snowmelt, have flooded the Dee valley; but other than in high-spate conditions, the Dee runs remarkably clear and is rarely severely coloured.

From time to time, sudden spates create an instant 'bore'; an independent wall of water, perhaps 3 ft high, travelling downstream at great speed. The noise of its approach should give ample warning to anglers wading in the river, but care should always be taken when fishing after heavy rain.

Notable Dee catches in recent years

(1987–1989)

WEIGHT	ANGLER	LOCATION
37 lb	David Jervis	Upper Drum
36 lb	Fred Fowler Jnr	Upper Drum
35 lb	Sgt Dave McDonald	Ardoe
31 lb 8 oz	John Fyfe	Kincaussie
30 lb 8 oz	John Lyndall	Raimore
29 lb	Pauline Kirkbride	Woodend
29 lb	Graham Reid	Kincaussie
29 lb	Mr Lankshear	Potarch
28 lb 8 oz	Woosey and Main	Banchory
28 lb	Brain Giles	Banchory
27 lb	Willie Donald	Raimore
27 lb	Donald Pirie	Ardoe
27 lb	John Green	Balnacoil
26 lb 8 oz	Abigail Hubbard	Balnacoil
26 lb 8 oz	Andrew Wright	Ballater
26 lb 8 oz	Ernst Stietzer	Raimore
26 lb	John Hodgson	Potarch
26 lb	Martin Buchan	Kincaussie
26 lb	Dan Dowell	Potarch
25 lb	David Lenton	Potarch
25 lb	Dan Dowell	Potarch
25 lb	Mrs McMillan	Banchory
25 lb	Brig Bradford	Kincardine
25 lb	Kath Strutt	Banchory
25 lb	David Iron	Raimore
24 lb	Brian Giles	Banchory
24 lb	Ralph Sampson	Aboyne
23 lb 8 oz	David Hay	Ardoe
23 lb	Douglas Gordon	Aboyne

WEIGHT	ANGLER	LOCATION
23 lb	Major-General Wilson	Banchory
23 lb	Robert Barnett	Aboyne
22 lb 8 oz	Mark Forrestor	Potarch
22 lb 8 oz	Edward Fordham	Banchory
22 lb	Robert Barnett	Aboyne
21 lb	David Bradey	Ardoe
21 lb	Wolfgang Reiss	Ballater
21 lb	Captain Green	Potarch
21 lb	Norman Jones	Banchory
21 lb	Mr Markland	Ballater
21 lb	David Blanch	Potarch
20 lb 8 oz	Ally Dodds	Kincaussie
20 lb	Ken Ray	Potarch

Downstream from Mar Lodge are the Invercauld and Balmoral fishings, including many fine pools and runs where salmon lie. The river here is particularly attractive and of modest size, being some 50 yards wide, and most of the lies can be covered easily from the bank.

ARTHUR WOOD'S SALMON

Ballater, a busy, bustling little town, is a favourite fishing centre, close to such famous beats as Lower Invercauld, Abergeldie, Birkhall, Monaltrie and Glen Muick; but the most famous fish is in the centre of town, rather than in the river: the cast of a magnificent salmon in the fishing-tackle shop, Country Wear, in Bridge Street, which used to be a saddler's. The salmon weighed 42 lb and was caught by Arthur Wood on June 18, 1926, and landed by his gillie, Tom Macphearson, of Invercauld Estate.

Arthur Wood was probably the most successful Dee salmon fisherman, and for a number of years leased the Cairnton Fishings, one of the finest of Dee's 45 salmon beats. From 1913 until 1934 A H Wood landed a total of 3,490 salmon, but he is best known as the inventor of the revolutionary greased-line method of salmon-fishing.

This technique was employed during low-water conditions and involved using a line, greased to make it float, and a small fly, quite the opposite of traditional tactics then used on Dee. Wood's success with the new method was instantly publicised and brought him great notoriety. For miles around, anglers followed suit, fishing a greased line with a small fly called the Blue Charm.

But not everyone agreed, and Jimmy Ross, who worked as a gillie on the Dee when he was a young man, knew Arthur Wood's gillie and reports him as saying: 'Don't believe it. It was a great big Jock Scott doing all the work, and everyone lashing away with these wee Blue Charms!'

The heaviest salmon ever caught on Dee was taken by another famous gillie, J Gordon, on the Ardoe Water in 1886. It weighed 57 lb 8 oz, although, as with so many of these 'ancient' fish, the weight is open to dispute. However, there is no dispute about the salmon caught on the Park Water on October, 1917: a fine specimen weighing 52 lb and the official record for the river.

Each season upwards of 8,000 salmon are caught. Sea-trout also run the river and provide great sport, although their numbers are rarely accurately recorded. In some years as many as 13,000 salmon have been landed. Numbers of salmon were severely affected in the late 1960s and early '70s when thousands of fish died, victims of UDN; since then, although still occurring, the disease seems to have declined.

The average weight of Dee salmon is in the order of 8 lb, and the best fishing is undoubtedly during the spring, when the main runs take place. Fewer fish enter the river during summer and autumn, but, as is the case with most Scottish rivers, these back-end fish are considerably larger than their spring cousins; not as huge as the legendary greybacks of south-west Scotland, or the mighty autumn fish of Tweed or Tay, but salmon of more than 20 lb and, occasionally, fish of even greater weight.

Ballater was developed by the Farquharson's in the late eighteenth century, when visitors came to the town to sample the waters from the health-giving springs at Pannanich. Such was the popularity of the area that it was planned to extend the railway up the glen to Braemar. It is said that Queen Victoria was 'not amused' by the prospect of her royal peace being disturbed, and the line was stopped at Ballater.

MAGNIFICENT WOODLANDS

Three major tributaries join Dee between Ballater and Aboyne: from the north, the Gairn, near the luxurious Craigendarroch Country Club; the Muick, flowing from deep Loch Muick and the dark corries of Lochnagar past the Queen Mother's home at Birkhall; and the delightful Water of Tanar, sweeping down from the wilderness of Mount Keen (939 m), past Shiel of Glentana and through magnificent woodlands to join the Dee near Bridge of Ess.

The banks of Dee and the surrounding hills are lined with fine Scots pine and birch, mixed with oak, ash, rowan, alder and willow, crowding the busy A93 road, built along the route of General Wade's old military road.

In days past, timber production was a major Deeside industry. Trees were floated down to the Aberdeen mills, and in 1822 this lead to disaster at Portarch Bridge, near Banchory. The bridge, which had been built only nine years previously, was demolished when jammed logs built up beneath the graceful arches and their weight brough the structure tumbling down.

Perhaps, after the accident, the 'floaters', as the river men were known, repaired to the Potarch Inn to drown their sorrows; as anglers do today, when fishing fates are unkind and salmon refuse to rise in the superb pool below the bridge.

At the entrance to the inn are two huge stones,

GRUINARD RIVER. Looking upstream from Gruinard Bay the wild and inhospitable An Teallach (1062 m) dominates the horizon. The river bubbles over stoney rapids through deserted moorlands where call of curlew is carried on the wind.

RIVER DEE. Captain Alwyne Farquharson with his keepers and their dogs on the Baddoch Beat on his Invercauld Estate. The official record of the largest salmon from Dee was one of 52 lb taken on Park Water in 1922.

Above
LOCH AWE. Fishing around these northern islands can provide the salmon angler with first class sport. It is a water to be respected as winds can turn it into a sea of white waves. Always head for cover if winds get up, the fish will always be there tomorrow.

Left
RIVER DON. This beautiful 2 lb 8 oz brown trout was caught by Bruce Sandison on Monymusk Waters from the Dam Pool. Other anglers in search of brown trout along this stretch often return anything under 2 lb . . . .

LOCH FADA. This is one of the Storr Lochs lying to the nort of Portree. It offers the best brown trout fishin on Skye. Baskets of ove ten fish are common. F on the horizon stands t needle shaped Old Mar of Storr.

each embedded with an iron ring, and each weighing 400 lb, perhaps used as anchors by the loggers. It is said that a local athlete, Donald Dinnie, once carried them, one in each hand, across Portarch Bridge. No one since has ever emulated his feat.

Another feat is commemorated just above Potach, where the river is enclosed for the last time into a narrow gorge barely 15 ft wide. Caird Young is reputed to have leapt the gorge, while fleeing for his life. The narrows are still known as Caird Young's Leap.

GENTLE PASTURES

The best-known beats between Aboyne and Banchory are Woodend and Cairnton on the north bank, and Commonty and Blackhall on the south bank; downstream from Banchory are such famous waters as Crathies, Invery, Park, Durris and Drum.

Below Aboyne, the river loses its distinctly Highland character, flowing sweetly through gentle pastures and fine farmlands; but it is nonetheless attractive, and all these beats can produce outstanding sport. It is just a matter of being in the right place at the right time – the salmon angler's constant dream.

At Dinnet, near to the Deeside Gliding Club airfield, the Dee District Fishery Board has a hatchery, and fry are planted out into the Dee's tributaries.

Until the 1870s the Dee was extensively netted, as far upstream as Banchory, where 16 stations reaped their deadly harvest of returning fish. Thereafter, largely due to the efforts of the Marquis of Huntly, descendant of the famous second Marquis, executed for his support of King Charles I in the Civil Wars of the fifteenth century, netting stations were bought and closed, until by 1968 only estuary nets remained. These have now gone and salmon have complete freedom of access river at all times.

And they are very particular about when they move, and where they rest. In early months, most fish seem to prefer the beats below Banchory; but by late April and early May they have moved upstream towards Aboyne and Ballater, and new fish entering the river often run straight through the lower beats to join their fellows further upstream.

Consequently, the lower beats are not very productive after April, and the chance of a salmon may depend upon placing a fly over the nose of a travelling fish. Obtaining the right to do so is just as difficult, for Dee fishing is highly prized and much sought-after.

The best beats are booked year after year by the same people, and most estates have waiting lists almost as long as the river itself. It is very much a question of 'dead-men's shoes', but it is always worth inquiring, well in advance, to see if there has perhaps been a cancellation.

JEWEL IN THE CROWN

Because of never-ending demand, weekly lets are the rule and a single day's fishing is hard to find. Nevertheless, a number of hotels have arrangements with owners, and the best opportunity for visiting anglers is to seek a booking through them.

In the spring, when the water is cold and fish lie deep, bait-fishing is allowed; although I believe that even then, a fly, properly fished, will bring just as good results. From April onwards, fly-only is the 'gentleman's' agreement, but, sadly, there is evidence that this rule is often broken.

Given the high cost of obtaining fishing, increasing number of anglers seem to be ready to resort to any method to catch fish; on the Dee, one of the classic fly-waters of the world, this is, in my opinion, little short of criminal.

The last stream to add its strength to Dee is the Water of Feugh, rising from the grouse moors and heather-clad slopes of Mount Battock (779 m), flowing softly through farmlands and deep pots to the famous falls near Banchory, where visitors gather to watch salmon leaping the torrent.

Banchory, often known as the Capital of Lower Deeside, is the centre for fishing the lower beats, and visiting anglers are well catered for by a number of excellent hotels, including Invery House, which has fishing rights on Water of Feugh and access to beats on the Dee.

North of the town is Hill of Fare, scene of the Battle of Corrichie, fought in 1562 between Mary, Queen of Scots, and the Gordons of Huntly; a mile from the site of the battle, on Berry Hill, is Queen's Chair, where Mary, from a safe distance, watched the progress of the fight. John Gordon, reputed to have been in love with Mary, was one of the casualties: Mary watched his head being removed from his shoulders a few days later in Aberdeen.

Today, less fiercesome battles rage on Deeside, between man and fish; and the quality of salmon fishing on the Dee is one of the principal angling joys of Scotland. There may be grander rivers and grander fish, but nothing compares with the excitement and pleasure of catching salmon in the cold, clear waters of this jewel in the Scottish angling crown.

10. The Don

LOCATION: Ordance Survey Landranger Series, 1:50,000. Sheets 36, Grantown and Cairngorm; 37, Strathdon; and 38, Aberdeen.

GRID REFERENCES: Sheet 36, Well of Don, 195067; Little Geal Charn. **Sheet 37**, Cock Bridge, 257090; Corgarff, 255087; Poldullie Bridge, 349124; Strathdon, 350125; Glenbucket Castle, 398149; Kildrummy Castle Hotel, 454164; Forbes Arms Hotel, 571172; Alfrod, 577161; Craigpot Suspension Bridge, 627188. **Sheet 38**, Paradise Wood, 677186; Grant Arms Hotel, Monymusk, 684153; Kemnay, 735160; Inverurie Bridge, 777207; Grandhome, 897120; Bridge of Don, 945097.

SEASONS: Salmon February 11–October 31; best months, March, April and October. Trout – March 15–September 30; best months May, June and September.

FLIES: Salmon – Munro Killer, General Practitioner, Scot's Special, Stoat's Tail, Corniehaugh, Shrimp Fly, Hairy Mary, Garry Dog; Thunder and Lightning. Trout – March Brown, Greenwell's Glory.

LURES: Sutherland Special, Yellow Sutherland, Yellow-belly Devon.

COSTS: Don salmon and trout fishing is not expensive and represents excellent value for money. The best beats cost about £20 per rod per day at prime times. Forbes Castle water is restricted to two rods per single-bank beat, and the estate gives preference to anglers who book the whole beat rather than single rods. Kildrummy fishing costs around £10 per rod per day, and day tickets are available. Glenkindie costs £40 per rod per week for salmon fishing.

Expect to pay between £20 and £40 per rod per week for brown-trout fishing. Costs on the lower Don are less, although the river tends to become crowded. The middle and upper beats offer a good degree of exclusiveness.

Excellent hotel and self-catering accommodation is available throughout the length of the river. Hotel charges vary from about £170 per week, full board at the Forbes Arms Hotel, Bridge of Alford, up to £300 per week at Kildrummy Castle. Well-furnished cottages cost £100/£180 per week, depending upon the time of year.

Full details of accommodation and other things to do and see in the area may be obtained from the Gordon and District Tourist Board, Tourist Information Centre, Railway Museum, Station Yard, Alford (Tel: 0336–2052), or the Area Tourist Officer, Inverurie Tourist Information Centre, Town Hall, Market Place, Inverurie (Tel: 0467–20600).

PERMISSION: Edinglassie, Candcraig And Glenkindie: Colquhonnie Hotel, Strathdon, Aberdeenshire. (Tel: 09756–51210).
Glenkindie: Glenkindie Hotel, Glenkindie, Strathdon, Aberdeenshire. (Tel: 09752–288).
Tornashean Water: Mr Mcintosh, Donview, Strathdon, Aberdeenshire. (Tel: 09752–302).
Kildrummy: T Hillary, Achnavenie, Kildrummy, Alford, Aberdeenshire. (Tel: 03365–208).
Alford: Forbes Arms Hotel, Bridge of Alford, Alford, Aberdeenshire. (Tel: 9755–62108).
Castle Forbes: Estate Office, Whitehouse, by Alford, Aberdeenshire. (Tel: 09755–62524).
Monymusk: Grant Arms Hotel, Monymusk, Aberdeenshire. (Tel: 04677–266).
Kemnay: F J & S L Milton, Kemnay House, Kemnay, Aberdeenshire. (Tel: 0467–42220).
Manor and Inverurie: J Duncan, 4 West High Street, Inverurie, Aberdeenshire. (Tel: 0467–20310); P Macphearson, Ironmonger, 49 Market Place, Inverurie. (Tel: 0467–21363).
Fintray: Aberdeen and District Angling Association, Messrs Clark & Wallace, Solicitors, 14 Albyn Place, Aberdeen. (Tel: 0224–64481).
Lower and Upper Parkhill: Jas Somers & Son, 40 Thistle Street, Aberdeen. (Tel: 0224–639910).
Grandhome: D Hunter, Mains of Grandhome, Woodside, Aberdeen. (Tel: 0224–723408).

RIVER DON. The chance of catching salmon of over 20 lb and brown trout of 4 lb plus draws anglers back year after year to do battle with this busy sparkling river. Few other Scottish rivers can offer as superb sport at such excellent value for money.

THE DON IS one of the finest salmon and trout streams in Europe, but quite unlike its close neighbour, the Dee, in character. While the Dee is a classic Highland spate stream, the Don takes a gentler view of life, ambling seawards to Aberdeen through fine farmlands from its wild Grampian beginnings. Ask an Aberdeenshire farmer for his opinion of the relative merits of the two rivers and he will probably reply: 'A mile o' Don's worth twa o' Dee'.

The river springs from Well of Don, on Little Geal Charn (709 m), to become the infant Feith Bhait stream, then the temperamental, adolescent Allt Tuileach – a high-banked, fast-flowing stream before joining with Meair Vennaich below Inchmore to reach adulthood, winding through heath and moorland to the fertile plains below.

Spring comes late to the gravelly, shallow upper Don. Kingcups, hazel, broom, pansies and forget-me-not have to be teased into bloom by the watery-yellow early summer sun. The heather landscape is scattered with boulders, bright with vivid, mustard-coloured lichens.

The cry of startled golden plover carries on the wind. Pied wagtails flit from stone to stone, piping their tune to wild brown trout which dart elusively in the strong current. When Schubert wrote his *Trout Quintet*, surely he must have had in mind a river very much like the delightful upper reaches of the Don.

The first major road to cross the Don is the A939, from Cockbridge to Tomintoul, which follows the line of one of General Wade's military roads, built during the early years of the eighteenth century. It is one of the best-known roads in Scotland, frequently featured in weather forecasts and famous for always being the first Scottish road to be blocked by winter snows.

One can easily imagine lines of weary red-coated soldiers, toiling up the steep slopes from Strathspey to the little hamlet of Tomintoul, the bayonets on their muskets glinting in evening sunlight; and their welcome pause for rest at the summit, glowered over by mighty Ben Macdhui. Now, the summit is occupied by taller sentinels, the stark, spider-web of ski-lifts and the untidy scatter of tea-rooms and cafes.

HAUNTING
HEATHER MOORS

On the south slope of this well-travelled path lies the gaunt, spectacular tower of Corgarff Castle. This granite-walled, grey-tiled building has had a long and turbulent history, matching the haunting surroundings of heather moors, spiked with Scots pine, stark and isolated in the white snows of winter. After the Earl of Mar's abortive rebellion in 1715, Corgarff was given to the Forbes family, in whose hands it remained until it was gifted to the nation.

The drove road which passed Corgarff Castle, connecting Angus with Inverness and the Moray Firth, was used by Montrose in 1645 during his brilliant campaign in support of Charles I. Less legal users crowded the narrow track, for the road was a favourite way of escape for Highlanders, herding back stolen lowland cattle to the safety of their wilderness homes in Badanoch and Lochaber.

At Cockbridge, the Don begins to grow from Highland burn into fully-fledged river, its banks decked with hazel, willow and yellow broom, crowded by pine-covered hillsides. The tree-line gives way to the high summits of grey, snow-capped Cairngorms from which tumbles busy Earran Water, close by Edingglassie House, another early eighteenth-century Forbes home.

Trees hug the river, making fishing difficult, but it is still possible to stalk the fine sporting trout which make fishing the higher reaches of the Don such a delight. This is excellent wet-fly water, sweeping past Candacraig House and under the bridge at Poldullie, a single-arched structure, 170 ft high, built in 1765 and still providing good service.

The Don flows swiftly into the Pot of Poldullie, a dark, secret pool where good trout lie, the banks alive with the song of birds calling from gentle woodlands that guard the stream.

Crystal-clear, snow-cold waters feed a salmon hatchery at Mill of Newe in Strathdon, helped by the Water of Nochty, cascading from the heights of the Ladder Hills (750 m). The hatchery carries up to 750,000 eggs each year. They are reared to the fry stage and then planted out in the headwaters of the river.

To the east lies Tornashean Forest, a dark conspiracy of conifers, breached by Deskry Water; and from here to a mile beyond Glenbucket Castle, the Don is often subjected to flooding when heavy rains combine with melting snows to send the river roaring in fury down the valley.

Glenbucket Castle, hedged in between the banks of the Don and Water of Bucket, is a ruined fortalice, originally belonging to the Gordon family, but subsequently bought by the Duffs, who built the imposing lodge at the north end of the glen.

Strathdon has a host of old castles, reminding the angler that in days past all was not peace and

RIVER DON. Looking downstream from Forbestown. Along the length of Don are over 60 beats to tempt anglers. The end of netting at the river mouth heralds a dazzling future for this water. Book well in advance.

tranquility as it is now; the ruins of Glenkindie; the site of sad Towie Castle, just upstream and dating from the sixteenth century, where Lady Forbes, her children and relations were burnt to death after the fight at Craibstone.

The only fights here now are between man and fish, and many a salmon has ended its days, gasping on the banks of this lovely stretch of the river.

Don flows serenely on, past the Peel Tower of Fichlie, perched on its 60 ft-high artificial mote-hill, near Cairn Fichlie, a Pictish round cairn from which no doubt in times past our ancestors sallied forth to net the river for returning fish.

THE GALLOWS

Downstream lies Kildrummy, one of the best of the upper Don salmon beats; and close by, the excellent Kildrummy Hotel, much-loved by anglers for many years. The ruins of Kildrummy Castle, built in the thirteenth century and dis-mantled after the 1715 rebellion, are among the most spectacular in Aberdeenshire; and it was here, in 1306, that Pembroke and the Comyns captured Nigel Bruce, brother of Robert Bruce, future King of Scotland.

Nigel Bruce was hanged, his entrails burnt before him, and then he was beheaded. The Earl of Atholl was also hanged, and because of his lofty, aristocratic lineage, he died on a gallows reputed to have been 30 ft tall, to match his high station in contemporary life.

At Bridge of Alford, the Don opens out into a substantial stream and the little hotel overlooking the banks of the river offers comfortable accommodation for anglers and excellent fishing within walking distance of the lounge-bar; useful if the fish are rising, and not too far to carry back the day's catch.

Bridge of Alford – pronounced Aaford – was the old centre before the coming of the railway, when a new town, called Alford was built; a long dismal straggling main street, famous for being the birthplace of Scottish poet, Charles Murray (1864–1941) and not much else.

The present bridge was built to replace the old ford and ferry, and this is one of the most scenic and attractive places to fish the Don. Downstream is Castle Forbes Estate, the ancestral seat of Lord Forbes, once known as Putachie – a gaelic word for trout.

It is an apt title, because Forbes Castle and Monymusk waters offer perhaps the finest brown-trout fishing in Scotland, the gem of which is Dam Pool, above Craigton Suspension Bridge, the best dry-fly water I have ever fished and home to trout of more than 6 lb.

Dam Pool still holds a good level of water even in summer conditions, and a feature of the river is the depth of some of the salmon holding pools. Wading always requires great caution, with deep unexpected pots waiting to catch you unawares.

THE RELIC OF
BANNOCKBURN

Dam Pool, like much of the river here, is fringed by tall weeds. These are cut in mid-summer, but not removed from the bank. It is easy to forget that they do not lie on *terra firma*, and anglers may be induced to take a dangerous step too far and find themselves having a much closer look at the pool than they originally intended. Caution is the watchword.

However, in low-water conditions it is possible

Notable catches in recent years

(1987–1989)

SALMON			BROWN TROUT		
WEIGHT	ANGLER	LOCATION	WEIGHT	ANGLER	LOCATION
27 lb	Ron Sutherland	Nether Don	4 lb 8 oz	Mike Cordiner	Monymusk
26 lb	Bert Webster	Grandhome	4 lb 4 oz	Bishop Holdernes	Forbes Castle
25 lb	Mike Cordiner	Monymusk	4 lb	Mr Surtees	Forbes Castle
24 lb	Ron Sutherland	Nether Don	3 lb 4 oz	Garry Bell	Monymusk
23 lb	Malcolm Whithead	Grandhome	3 lb 2 oz	Steve Whitton	Colquhonnie
19 lb 8 oz	Paul Merison	Grandhome	3 lb	Mike Aitken	Forbes Castle
19 lb 2 oz	Mr Eweing	Monymusk	3 lb	Keith Lord	Monymusk
19 lb	Allan Stones	Grandhome	2 lb 8 oz	Steven Whitton	Colquhonnie
18 lb 8oz	Francis Grant	Monymusk	2 lb 8 oz	Bruce Sandison	Monymusk
18 lb	Malcolm Bruce	Forbes Castle			
17 lb 8 oz	Adrian Latimer	Forbes Castle			
15 lb 8 oz	W Thomson	Inverurie			
15 lb 8 oz	Martin Evans-Bevan	Monymusk			
15 lb 8 oz	W Thomson	Torphins			
15 lb	Ken Taylor	Inverurie			
14 lb	J Milligan	Inverurie			
12 lb 8 oz	David Mair	Inverurie			

(A brown trout of 7 lb 12 oz was caught on Forbes Castle Water in 1985)

to wade down the north bank and cross the dam itself to reach the stream on the far bank, where good fish lie under the cover of overhanging branches – a test of casting skill, but well worth the effort.

One of the great delights of fishing the Don is the fact that if salmon are being unco-operative, then it is always possible to have good sport with trout – the best of all worlds; and an outstanding stretch of dry-fly water flows through superb Paradise Woods, a mile or so upstream from Monymusk.

The ancient trees were planted in 1719 by Lord Cullen, and the river here is alive with the hum of insects and the urgent splashes of rising trout.

Anglers come from all over the world to fish this stretch for brown trout, and fish of more than 3 lb are frequently taken. These dry-fly experts invariably return all fish under 2 lb, keeping only specimen trout as evidence of their skill.

The charming little village of Monymusk is another good angling centre from which to fish the middle Don. Colin Hart, an expert angler, runs the comfortable Grant Arms Hotel and takes good care of visiting anglers. The hotel has its own fishing rights on Don, including Paradise Wood, and each year Grant Arms Hotel guests take about 150 salmon – and fine baskets of brown trout.

Monymusk House, near the village, was built in 1587 and used to boast a relic of St Columba, a bone from his foot. This was kept in a seventh century casket, known as the Monymusk Requilary, and it was carried before the Scottish army at the Battle of Bannockburn in 1314.

The old house became the property of Sir Francis Grant, Lord Cullen, in 1712, and it was his son, Alexander Grant, who was the great tree-planter, establishing more than one million trees each year during a period of 50 years.

Spring and autumn provide the best sport with salmon, but much depends upon water levels; unlike the Dee, which has no obstacles to returning fish, Don salmon have obstructions to negotiate: Whyte's Dyke, above the Devil's Rock Pool, and the Cruives. Pollution is the lower reaches has also played havoc with stocks of fish, as has rampant poaching.

Pollution control has improved in recent years, but best news is that all netting at the river mouth has ended and returning salmon have freedom of access to their spawning grounds at all times. The activities of poachers are also being much curtailed, and there is every sign that the Don will soon regain its status as a major salmon river.

A FICKLE LADY

The river boasts 63 beats, and access for visiting anglers is readily available through local angling clubs, hotels and estates. While spring fishing is always in demand and well booked in advance, rods are generally available from May onwards, when sea-trout also enter the river and can provide great sport.

Sport with brown trout is best in May and June, and back-end salmon fishing can be really excellent, with large autumn fish surging upstream. The Don season extends into October, so when the rods are packed away on neighbouring Dee on September 30, many anglers end their season with a few days on Don.

From Monymusk, the Don winds slowly eastwards, collecting in the Urie, flowing past the old granite quarries at Kemnay, used during the construction of the Forth Railway Bridge.

Dowstream from Kemnay, the Don is a fickle lady, much given to bursting her banks in angry spate, continually cutting away at new channels, leaving the behind anxious ox-bows thick with weeds, snapdragons and sedges, and watering some of the best farmland in the north of Scotland.

The last 18 miles of the river, from Inverurie downstream, once served as a canal, built in 1807 and the remains of the mills and works that lined the banks can still be seen.

Before reaching Bridge of Don, in a final act of defiance, the sides of the river become steep again, enclosing pools which are often 25 ft or more deep; then the Don regains its composure, ending its 82-mile-long journey by slipping quietly over a sandbar into the cold waters of the North Sea.

11. The Hebrides

THE DELIGHTFUL ISLANDS of the Inner and Outer Hebrides offer some of the finest gamefishing in Scotland. They offer amazingly beautiful scenery, with something of interest for every member of the family; allowing fishermen to get on with their proper function in life.

Men have lived and worked on the Hebrides for more than 7,000 years and monuments to their endeavours abound throughout the islands: burial chambers, standing stones, stone circles, brochs, duns and forts, churches and castles.

In the sixth century, Columbus arrived from Ireland and established his monastery on the tiny island of Iona, off the west coast of Mull; and soon after, Harland Fairhair and his wild Norse tribes began their long domination of Scotland's west coast.

In 1165, Somerled, a descendent of the kings of Ireland, became Lord of the Isles, establishing the Clan Donald dynasty; finally, the young Scottish king, Alexander, defeated the Norsemen at the Battle of Largs in 1263, thus freeing the Hebrides from Viking domination.

But it took several hundred years more before the power of the Lords of the Isles was broken and Clan Donald was persuaded to recognise the King of Scotland's authority over the isles.

Battles still rage in the islands today, but they are mostly between man and fish, rather than between man and his fellows. Wherever you go in the Hebrides, you will be assured of a warm welcome and great sport.

LOCATION: Ordnance Survey Second Series, 1:50,000.

SKYE: Sheets 23, North Skye, and 32, South Skye.

GRID REFERENCES: Sheet 23, Ose, 314411; Snizort, 420484.

MULL: Sheets 49, Oban and East Mull; 48, Iona and Ben More; 47, Tobermory.

GRID REFERENCES: Sheet 47, Aros River, 557448; Forsa River, 596427, Loch Frisa, 490485, Mishnish Lochs, 480526; **Sheet 48**, Loch Assapoll, 405205; **Sheet 49**, Lussa River, 685307.

ISLAY: Sheet 60, Islay.

GRID REFERENCES: Gorm Loch, 230660.

JURA: Sheet 61, Jura and Colonsay.

GRID REFERENCE: Lussa River, 645870.

ARRAN: Sheet 69, Island of Arran.

GRID REFERENCE: 894330 Nachrie Water.

LEWIS AND HARRIS: Sheets 8, Stornoway and North Lewis; 13, West Lewis and North Harris; 14, Tarbert and Loch Seaforth; 18, Sound of Harris.

GRID REFERENCES: Sheet 8, Grimersta, 213296; Blackwater, 235301; River Creed, 416320; **Sheet 13**, River Laxay, 316218; Loch Valtos, 315212; Uig Lodge, 056334; Amhuinnsuidhe, 043084; **Sheet 13**, The Obbe, 015869.

BENBECULA AND UISTS: Sheets 18, Sound of Harris; 22, Benbecula; 31, Barra.

GRID REFERENCES: Sheet 18, Loch Skeltar, 895687; Loch nan Geireann, 850720; **Sheet 22**, Ba Alasdair, 857495; Grogarry Loch, 762395; Stilligarry Loch, 765380; West Loch Ollay, 740327.

SEASONS: Salmon and sea-trout fishing in the Hebrides is generally from mid-February until the end of September, although on some systems the season extends into the first two weeks of October. Spring runs of salmon are sparse and the best sport is to be had during autumn.

ISLAND OF Harris. The landscape is jewelled with lochs and lochans teeming with wild brown trout. You can almost be certain that you will not meet another person all day in this remote wilderness.

It is possible to catch sea-trout in the sea off much of the Hebridean coasts as early as March and April; but sea-trout don't run the rivers until late June and early July. Late July and August are usually the most productive months.

Brown-trout fishing opens on March 15, but sport is poor until the water temperature rises. May can often be superb, and June is probably the best month. September can also be excellent.

FLIES: Hebridean salmon seem to prefer well-dressed flies, although the exceptions prove the rule. Offer them: Kate Mclaren, Garry dog, Goat's Toe, Munro Killer, Shrimp Fly, Green Highlander, Hairy Mary, Silver Wilkinson, General Practitioner and Waddingtons.

Sea-trout will often take the salmon flies named above, and salmon frequently take sea-trout and brown-trout patterns. It makes fishing in the Hebrides that much more interesting than in other places; you never really know what has grabbed hold until you get a good look at it.

Offer sea-trout and brown trout: Ke-He, Soldier Palmer, Black Pennell, Loch Ordie, Black Zulu, Blue Zulu, Charlie Maclean, Invicta, Grouse and Claret, Grouse and Green, March Brown, Greenwell's Glory, Dunkeld, Peter Ross, Alexandra, Gold Butcher, Silver Butcher.

COSTS: Costs vary widely. The best of the salmon fishing, if obtainable at all, will, cost up to £8,000 for a week. Having said that, excellent fishing is often available on lesser rivers from £12 to £30 per rod per day; and if you are there after a good spate, then you may do just as well as anglers on the more-famous beats.

Sea-trout fishing can also be expensive: the North Harris Estate charges £15,000 for one week, with a maximum of 12 rods fishing. Less expensive sea-trout fishing can be found in the sea-pools of North Uist; and loch fishing for sea-trout will cost in the region of £12 to £25 per day for a boat with two rods fishing.

Brown-trout fishing is rarely expensive, although to obtain access to the best fishing, such as the machair lochs of South Uist, you have to stay at the Lochboisdale Hotel.

A week's hotel accommodation, with full board and fishing, will cost between £200 and £380 per week. Bed-and-breakfast accommodation is generally readily available throughout the Hebrides at about £18–£25 per person per night, with evening meal; self-catering cottages cost £150–£250 per week.

PERMISSION:

SKYE Ose and Snizort: Skeabost House Hotel, Skeabost Bridge, Skye (Tel: 047032–202); Ullinish Lodge Hotel, Struan, Skye (Tel: 047072 214).
Storr Lochs and Other Skye Lochs and Rivers: Skye Angling Club, Masonic Buildings, Portree, Skye (Tel: 0478–204).

MULL Most Rivers and Lochs: Tackle & Boots, Tobermory, Isle of Mull (Tel: 0688–2336).
Loch Assapoll: James Mckeand, Scoor House, Bunessan, Mull. (Tel: 06817–297).

ISLAY Gorm Loch: B Wiles, Islay House, Bridgend, Islay, Argyll (tel: 049681 293).
Other Lochs: The Port Askaig Shop, Port Askaig, Islay, Argyll (Tel: 049684–633).

JURA: Lussa River and Loch: C Fletcher, Ardlussa Estate, Ardlussa, Jura, Argyll (Tel: 049682–323).

ARRAN Most Rivers and Lochs: A J Andrews, The Secretary, Arran Angling Club, Park House, Arran.

LEWIS AND HARRIS General Information: The Sports Shop, 6 North Beach Street, Stornoway, Isle of Lewis (Tel: 0851–5464).
BENECULA AND THE UISTS NORTH UIST: Department of Agriculture, Area Office, Balavanich, Benbecula (Tel: 0870 2346); and Lochmaddy Hotel, Lochmaddy, North Uist (Tel: 08963–331).
BENBECULA AND SOUTH UIST: The Secretary, South Uist Angling Club, Balavanich, Benbecula; and Captain John Kennedy, the Lochboisdale Hotel, Lochboisdale, South Uist (Tel: 08784–332).

Skye

THE MISTY ISLAND of Skye is soon to be joined to mainland Scotland by a new bridge across the narrows at Kyle of Lochalsh. The project has been received with mixed feelings on the island. Many foresee the end of the old, Highland way of life, with the island becoming increasingly dominated by tourism.

Skye is inextricably linked with Bonnie Prince Charlie, who escaped from Benbecula in 1746, arriving on Skye still dressed as Betty Burke, Flora Macdonald's 'maid'. Dr Johnson and Boswell had dinner with Flora Macdonald and her husband at Kingsburgh during their tour of the Highlands, and Johnson was enraptured by Flora's charm and fortitude.

Because of its accessibility, Skye is a busy island, popular with visitors from all over the world. Many come to climb in the Cuillin Hills, considered to be as challenging as the Alps, and for decades the training ground for Scottish climbers. Others simply enjoy the beauty of their surroundings and are content to while away lazy days by loch or river, wandering over the verdant, green hills, or dozing summer afternoons away beside an incredibly blue sea.

The best fishing on Skye is controlled by hotels. Ullinish Lodge and Skeabost House Hotel both have access to the Rivers Snizort and Ose, which can provide excellent sport with salmon and sea-trout. But they are very much spate streams, and will produce of their best only after heavy rain. Fortunately, Skye is also famous for stormy, wet weather, so the chances of being in the right place at the right time are always high.

July and August are good months, but you are advised to book well in advance. The Snizort and Ose are popular among a small, knowledgeable group of anglers, and people return year after year to fish these lovely little rivers.

Other spate-river fishing for salmon and sea-trout is available on the Kilmartin, Kilmalug, Lealt and Conon rivers. The best brown-trout fishing is on the Storr Lochs, to the north of Portree.

Skye may not offer the best fishing in Scotland, but it most certainly offers quality sport among outstanding surroundings. Few places can match the beauty and serenity of the lovely Misty Isle.

Mull

MULL IS AN island of gentle mountains, pine forests, deserted beaches and wild, lovely moorlands. The highest peak is mighty Ben More (966 m), famous as the site of the world's most celebrated fossil tree, preserved in Ben More's lava flows millions of years ago.

The main population centre is graceful Tobermory, home to the Mull Highland Games, held in a natural amphitheatre on the hillside near the town. More serious games were held in Bloody Bay, to the north, in 1439; the scene of a sea-battle when the Macleans of Mull supported John Argyll, forth Lord of the Isles, against his son, Angus.

The Macleans' principal residence on Mull was dramatic Duart Castle, on the south-east coast, confiscated after the 1745 Rebellion. The Macleans were staunch Jacobites and paid heavily for their support of Prince Charles Edward Stewart.

Like most of the Hebrides, Mull offers good spate-river fishing for salmon and sea-trout on a number of delightful streams. The trick is to be there after heavy rain.

The Aros River flowing into the Sound of Mull close to Aros Castle, where Lord Ochiltree met the Hebridean chiefs in 1608. King James VI was determined to bring order to the islands, and Ochiltree, acting upon James's instructions, trapped the chiefs on board a warship. They were transported to Edinburgh Castle and incarcerated there until they promised to behave; which,

eventually, most of them did.

The most famous pool of Aros River is Ash Tree Pool, where, in 1911, a 45 lb salmon was taken. Today's salmon are somewhat smaller, averaging about 7 lb. The main run comes in July, depending upon weather conditons, and most seasons produce upwards of 100 fish.

The Aros is also a noted sea-trout fishery, from late June right through to the end of the season. The fish average 1 lb 8 oz, although most seasons produce a few sea-trout of more than 3 lb.

The Lussa can also offer great sport with salmon and sea-trout. It is a bustling stream, its cascading waters swirling seawards between conifer-lined banks and entering Loch Spelve, an almost enclosed sea loch.

The best fishing is on the lower River, wait for the spate, book a day, and look out for action, particularly in mysterious Pedlar's Pool. The salmon average about 8 lb and the sea-trout run up to 3 lb. The Lussa is the best of the Mull salmon streams available to visiting anglers.

The Forsa, another stream to flow into the Sound of Mull, gathers its strength from the heights of Beinn Talaidh (2,502 ft), Sgurr Dearg (2,429 ft), Dun Ghaoithe (2,512 ft) and Beinn Chreagach (1,903 ft). A track leads from the A849, close to Mull Airport, upstream to Tomsleibhe, giving access to the upper reaches.

The river is a delight of small pools and tumbling rapids, with always the chance of a fish. New delights beckon around each bend, and part of the great pleasure of fishing this stream is stalking the fish; keeping well back from the bank, crouching below the skyline, fingers crossed.

Loch Frisa, Mull's largest loch, can also provide excellent sport. It has been stocked in recent years with a strain of Loch Leven brown trout. Boat fishing, particularly round the margins, brings best results and trout average 12 oz.

Frisa flows into the Aros and from time to time, salmon find their way into the loch. They are rarely caught, but you never know your luck. One final word of warning regarding Frisa; it can be a wild and windy water. Seek local advice before setting out, and never take any chances with the weather.

Assapoll is a first-class fishery, nestling in remote moorlands on the Ross of Mull, at the south of the island, near the road to Iona. It offers outstanding sport with salmon, sea-trout and brown trout – a loch for all seasons. Both boat and bank fishing is available, and the main runs of salmon and sea-trout come with high tides in late July.

The salmon average about 8 lb, the grilse 5 lb and sea-trout 2 lb. Brown trout can be caught all season, and they average 12 oz, although fish of up to 7 lb have been taken. This is one of the most delightful lochs in Scotland, amid glorious scenery, and is well worth a visit. Self-catering and serviced accommodation is available, linked to the fishing.

Alternative trout-fishing is readily available on Mull, but the best of it is on the Mishnish Lochs, three inter-linked waters lying between Dervaig and Tobermory.

The lochs are regularly stocked and are different in character. Pellach is shallow and sometimes weedy, but contains trout of more than 2 lb; Meadhoin is the nursery, teeming with small fish; and Carnain an Amis will make you work hard for a brace of 1 lb fish – but they will be of superb quality. There's something for everyone.

Islay

ISLAY IS THE ancient seat of the Lords of the Isles, from which they ruled their Hebridean domains for 500 glorious years. Its salmon-fishing is mostly private, with few opportunities for visiting anglers. However, fishing for wild brown trout is readily available.

The best of the trout fishing is in the north of the island, where the Gorm Loch will provide excellent sport. Baskets of up to 12 fish are frequently taken, with boat-fishing bringing best results. But the loch is shallow and rocky, so hasten slowly, and take spare sheer-pins for the outboard motor.

Jura

JURA MEANS 'THE island of deer', and, indeed, the island is one of the most noted stalking areas in Europe. It has only one road, which winds up the east coast of the island to finish at the cottage where George Orwell completed his sad masterpiece, *1984* shortly before his death.

Northwards from Orwell's cottage is the famous Gulf of Corryvrechan, with its notorious whirlpool, which nearly robbed the world of *1984*. The sound of its roaring waters can be heard from a considerable distance, and it is one of the few places off Britain's coasts that the Royal Navy classifies as un-navigable.

Western Jura is a trackless wilderness, home to eagle, wildcat and otter, guarded by remote, vast cliffs and deserted tiny bays, where the only way in is by foot across the morland and mountains.

Fishing on Jura is mainly with brown trout, but salmon and sea-trout fishing may be available from time to time on the Lussa, a spate stream on the east coast which relies heavily on rain and high tides to produce of its best; but then sport may be very good. A loch at the head of the river can give great fun, particularly with sea-trout, when the river runs low.

Jura is a magical island and, regardless of the quality of fishing, a delightful place to escape from the slings and arrows of outrageous fortune. After a good downpour, it is even better.

Arran

ARRAN IS A lovely island, popular with visitors from the west of Scotland and dominated by Goat Fell (2,868 ft) and the 'sleeping warrior'. Viewed from the east, the mountains take on the shape of a huge man, lying on his back, knees slightly bent.

Arran has had a turbulent past. In 1335, after breaking the Treaty of Northampton, Edward III, supporting the Balliol claim to the throne of Scotland, paid a visit – with 50 ships and 1,500 armed men. Robert Stewart, for the time being, bowed to the inevitable; but eventually he ousted Edward's siblings and became Robert II of Scotland, founder of the House of Stewart.

Gamefishing on Arran is not outstanding, although the scenery most certainly is. Nevertheless, the delightful Machrie Water can offer superb sport, given the right water conditions. Here, during the short July nights, salmon and sea-trout slip quiely past the Machrie Moor standing stones, heading upstream to their gravelly spawning burns in the high hills. Up to 50 are caught each year at an average of 6 lb, along with good numbers of sea-trout. The hours of darkness are the best time to fish.

Lewis

SEEN FROM AN aircraft, 'Long Island' resembles a tree leaf floating in the Atlantic and sprinkled with silver raindrops. It is a wild, desolate land, covered with peat to the north and east, fringed with glorious, golden beaches along the western edges.

The island has hundreds of trout lochs, from tiny pools to long, wild waters which will test your stamina and map-reading to the limit if you are to reach them, and all contain hard-fighting fish which vary in size from a few inches right up to 'monsters' of 6 lb and more.

Most of the island is owned by a few large estates which jealously guard their salmon and sea-trout fishing. What little salmon-fishing is available to visitors is generally booked well in advance and is very expensive.

Nor is there any guarantee of catching anything; most Lewis streams are spate systems; no water, no fish. It is always advisable, if booking, to ask to see previous years' catch-returns before making you decision.

Having said that, if weather conditions are kind – that is, very wet – then you may have excellent sport in Lewis. The Grimersta, on the west coast, is less-affected by water levels because of a system of dams which control the flow. Grimersta is probably one of the most prolific salmon rivers in the world. It holds the world record for the most salmon taken on fly during a single day: 57 fish. Autumn produces best results, but it is impossible to obtain fishing then.

But spring fishing is sometimes available, and it, too, can be first-class. Guests at Grimersta during May and June in recent years have mixed fortunes, some weeks producing up to 50 salmon, others none at all. It is all part of the lottery of salmon-fishing.

The system is divided into four beats: Beat 4, from where the river leaves Loch Langavat into Loch Airgh na h-Airde; Beat 3, containing Loch Faoghail Charrasan; Beat 2, the connecting stream from Loch Faoghail Charrasan and the southern half of Loch Faoghail an Tuim; and Beat 1, half Grimersta and half Loch Faoghail an Tuim.

MAGICAL FISHING

It is magical fishing and well worth plotting, planning, saving, robbing, murder and mayhem to obtain a week. Pools on the Grimersta to raise your blood-pressure are Bridge, Captain's, Sea Pool and Battery Pool. It could be that week to remember.

But while Grimersta is the best of the Lewis fishing, several other systems which can also produce good sport, given decent water levels.

The Blackwater River, to the north of Grimersta, is an excellent salmon stream with fish averaging 7 lb and upwards of 100 taken each season. Its headwater lochs have been dammed to provide freshets in dry weather, and the the river has a series of delightful runs and pots where salmon lie, particularly in the last mile or so to the sea at Loch Roag, guarded by the famous Callanish standing stones.

The island of Vuia Beag, in Loch Roag, is reputed to have magical powers which attract salmon, and it is known locally as 'salmon run'.

RIVER GRIMERSTA. This is probably one of the most prolific salmon rivers in the world. Best fishing is in autumn but impossible to obtain. Other weeks available may give 50 fish or none.

Salmon are reputedly drawn to the little island during a full moon and may spend several hours circling it before escaping from its spell and continuing their journey upstream.

The little River Laxy is another excellent Lewis salmon stream. The best sport is had on Loch Valtos, half-a-mile upstream from the sea at Loch Erisort. Autumn offers the best opportunities on this lovely water, and most seasons produce about 200 salmon and 300 sea-trout. The salmon average 7 lb, although in 1933 a fine fish of 33 lb 8 oz was caught. Sea-trout average 1 lb 8 oz.

PRINCE CHARLIE'S CAIRN

The Laxy system is divided into three beats, with boat fishing on Loch Valtos. Top, Middle and Lower river all have good holding pools, one of the best of which is Reedy Pool.

At Stornoway is the River Creed. It flows into Stornoway Harbour Bay near Prince Charlie's Cairn, a monument to Charles Edward, who tried, unsuccessfully, to purchase a boat in Stornoway during his travels round the Outer Hebrides after the disaster at Culloden in 1746.

Close by is Breasts of Holm, site of Scotland's greatest maritime tragedy when, on January 1, 1919, *HMY Iolaire* foundered, drowning almost 200 soldiers and sailors returning home after the Great War.

The Creed's salmon and sea-trout run from July onwards, peaking during August and September, the river taking them through Lady Lover's park, with its marvellous display of rhododendrons, and up a narrow gorge to the gravelly pools below Loch an Ois. The salmon average 6 lb and the sea-trout about 1 lb 8 oz. The river is divided into three beats, with only one rod being allowed to fish each beat at any one time. Junction, Falls and Bond Pools can all give fine sport, as can the lochs at the head of the system.

The last of the notable Lewis salmon-fishing systems is set amid perhaps the most beautiful surroundings, at Uig, with magnificent, shining-white beaches, backed by a range of wild mountains. It was here that the famous Lewis chessmen were found; disturbed by a cow rubbing itself against the sand dunes. The pieces are carved out of walrus ivory and date from the twelfth century. They are now safely displayed in the Queen Street Museum, Edinburgh, and the British Museum, London.

The Uig fishery is very much a spate system and water-flow is sometimes non-existent in dry summer months; but even then, Loch Suainval, famous for its legendary water-horse, generally provides sport. One of the Lords of Seaforth's gillies once claimed to have been chased by the water-horse after his barking dogs had disturbed the monster's slumber. The gillie escaped, but his hounds were found dead on the moor next morning.

Loch Suainval is a deep, long loch, extending for nearly four miles and being a quarter-of-a-mile wide. A grid at the outlet of the loch keeps salmon in the short river, and is removed only at spawning time to allow the fish into the cold waters of the loch.

THE LOVE OF LEWIS

Uig Lodge, built by Lord Leverhume, stands on a grassy knoll overlooking the sands, and anglers fishing the system stay in the lodge during their let of the river.

Brown-trout fishing on Lewis deserves a book to itself. With hundreds of lochs from which to choose, you will usually have one to yourself. To see other anglers is the exception rather than the rule.

The best time to fish for brown trout in Lewis is late May and June, although good sport can be had throughout the season. Loch Langavat, the largest freshwater loch in the island, contains salmon and sea-trout as well, and is a wonderful water on which to spend a day, with plenty of 'fishy corners' and lovely bays.

Trout fisherman instantly fall in love with Lewis. Several lifetimes' fishing are scattered through the moorland and mountain; and no visitor ever has enough time to do justice to it all. The best advice for prospective visitors is to get started as soon as possible. Don't lose a moment.

Harris

THE WILD, RUGGED landscape of Harris is in complete contrast to that of its northern neighbour, Lewis. It is almost impossible to describe the astonishingly desolate nature of this distant land. Hundreds of lochs lie scattered in the hills, and the beaches, white crescents of deserted sand, are among the most stunning in the world. The sea is often vivid blue, shading to emerald and green, reflecting the clear skies and heather-clad hills. It is a wonderland of delight.

Harris is divided into two. North Harris continuous with Lewis, and South Harris is connected to it by a narrow neck of land at Tarbert. It is in the north that the best fishing is to be found, at Amhuinnsuidhe. Here a magnificent grey-stone Victorian lodge dominates the bay, and in the hills beyond is salmon and sea-trout fishing to rival the best anywhere.

Unfortunately for most anglers, the costs involved match the quality of sport. A week's accommodation, complete with full board, fishing, gillies and transport to the lochs, will cost in the order of £15,000 for a party of 15.

THE HAUNT OF THE FAIRIES

Most seasons produce upwards of 200 salmon, and in 1989, 1,400 sea-trout were caught. The salmon average about 7 lb, and the sea-trout run up to 4 lb. In spite of the price, there is no lack of people wishing to fish the North Harris Estate waters, so if you can muster a group of angling friends who are looking for the best possible sport,

HARRIS. One of the delights of fishing here is that you are certain to catch fish. No prayers or rain dances are necessary before you go. Just lose yourself in the mystical beauty of it all.

make inquiries early. Amhuinnsuidhe will provide superb sport in an outstanding location.

South from Amhuinnsuidhe, at Leverburgh, lies the Borve Estate, which has salmon and sea-trout fishing on the Obbe system. The two principal lochs, Steisevat and Loch na Moracha, are both easily accessible and worth a cast.

Close by is Dun Borve, reputed haunt of fairies, released from captivity by a sailor who removed an iron sword from a stone. In return for their freedom, the fairies gave the man a magic stone for grinding salt; but his companions stole the stone and murdered its owner. That was their bad luck. The stone continued grinding away until the boat filled with salt and sank, drowning everyone in the process.

Brown-trout fishing on Harris is not as good as on Lewis, and the fish tend to be much smaller. But size is never important to true anglers, and one of the great delights of fishing on Harris is the certain knowledge that you will easily catch breakfast for the following day.

Benbecula and the Uists

NORTH UIST, BENBECULA and South Uist are an anglers' paradise; and no fishing career is complete without a pilgrimage to these lovely, sparkling Hebridean isles. The three islands, with Benbecula between the two Uists, are now linked by causeways, making access easy, and their western edge is an almost continuous beach of golden sands backed by fertile, green fields known as 'machair'.

In spring and early summer the machair blossoms into a riot of wild flowers, washed by endless, blue Atlantic waves. Golden eagle and buzzard lord the skies, and each loch seems to have its own resident flock of graceful mute swans.

The islands have been inhabited for thousands of years and the homes of ancient Man lie scattered among the bleak moorlands: duns, huge mounds of tumbled stones, perched on small promontories by the shores of lochs; burial chambers, still well preserved; and wheelhouses, in use from first century BC right up until the times of the Vikings.

The exploits of these early inhabitants are remembered in the names of their burns, hills and streams. Carinish, at the south end of North Uist, was the site of the last clan battle, when the Macleods of Harris fought the Macdonalds of Uist. The dead were unceremoniously thrown into a nearby ditch which is to this day known as 'Feithe na Fala', the 'Ditch of Blood'.

The most famous visitor to the isles was Bonnie Prince Charlie, hiding from his pursuers after defeat at the Battle of Culloden. The Prince landed first on Benbecula and for several weeks played a game of cat-and-mouse through the islands, deperately trying to find a means of escape back to mainland Scotland.

His principal hiding place was in a cave on the wild, trackless east coast of South Uist, near Loch Hellisdale, beyond Beinn Mhor. Eventually, as the net tightened, and 2,000 Government troops descended on Benbecula to hunt for the fugitive, Lady Clanranald devised the means for his escape, dressed as Flora Macdonald's maid, Betty Burke.

BARS OF SHINING SILVER

Fishing on North Uist and Benbecula is managed by the Lochmaddy Hotel and the Department of Agriculture. The islands have dozens of excellent wild brown-trout lochs and several good sea-trout systems. But the only salmon fishing of note is on the Skelter system, where, since the removal of a fish-farming enterprise, the loch is rapidly regaining its status as a prime salmon fishery.

Loch Skelter is one of a chain of lochs which drain eastwards to the sea at Loch Maddy. Salmon arrive in late February and about 100 fish averaging about 5 lb are caught each season, Uist salmon are rarely larger. Sea-trout also run the system, and they average 1 lb 8 oz.

A single road circles North Uist, and at the north end of the island lies one of the most exciting Uist waters, Loch Nan Geireann. This long, straggling water, is home to hundreds of beautifully marked wild brown trout, as well as salmon and sea-trout; so, no matter where you fish, there is always the chance of hooking something special.

Geireann flows northwards, and at low tide a vast area of white sand is exposed, swallowing the course of the little river; but across the sands, close to the sea, is a marvellous, tidal pool which is one of the most beautiful and exciting places to fish.

Salmon and sea-trout, like bars of shining silver, leap and splash in the clear waters; and to many the thrill of catching these fighting fish in such natural surroundings is the pinnacle of angling achievement.

Other sea-pools may be found down the west coast of North Uist; but great care should always be taken in approaching them. There are often quicksands, ready to catch the unwary, and anglers should seek local advice and directions before setting out.

South from Lochmaddy, along the shore of Loch Eport, are other locations where sea-trout may be caught in the sea, but most require a long, difficult hike across damp moor. Nevertheless, once there, most anglers agree that the effort involved in reaching these remote areas is well worth while.

One of the delights of fishing in the Hebrides is the wealth of birdlife to be seen; and few islands offer a greater variety than Benbecula and the Uists. The Balranald Nature Reserve, centred on marshy ground near Loch nam Feithean, hosts many rare species, including red-necked phalarope. To the south, at the north end of South

Uist, is the magnificent Loch Druidibeg Reserve, dominated by the graceful shape of Hecla (606 m), and Beinn Mhor (620 m), the highest peak on South Uist.

Benbecula, 'the hill of the fords', shows most signs of change. The military base at Balivanich, which services the South Uist rocket range, has brought considerable prosperity; and an excellent NAAFI, much patronised by the islanders.

Brown-trout fishing on Benbecula is excellent and there are a few locations where sea-trout may also be caught; principally at Loch Ba Alasdair, where the loch's outlet enters into the sea.

The best Hebridean fishing is on South Uist; for not only does the island boast some of the finest brown-trout lochs, but it also offers superb sport with sea-trout and salmon.

PEACE AND QUIET

The machair lochs fish well for trout from May onwards, with late May and June the most productive months. These shallow, lime-rich waters warm up quickly in the spring; but as the season advances, some of them become weedy. That's good news for trout, but bad news for anglers trying to catch them.

Grogarry Loch, at the north of the island, is reputed to hold the biggest fish, and trout of more than 3 lb are sometimes taken. Fish of 2 lb are the rule rather than the exception, and both boat and bank fishing bring excellent results.

Southwards from Grogarry are several other famous machair lochs: Stilligarry, West Loch Ollay, Bornish and Kildonan, all offering outstanding sport with fine quality, perfectly-shaped, pink-fleshed brown trout.

Sea-trout and salmon are caught in four

systems, centred on Lochs Fada, Roag, Howmore, Barph and East Loch Ollay. Although salmon rarely reach double figures in weight, excellent sea-trout are caught in most seasons. Pat Green, fishing Fada in 1989, had a magnificent fish weighing 8 lb. A Mr Cooke had a sea-trout of 7 lb 8 oz from Roag in September, 1989; and Barph and Howmore also produced a number of sea-trout of more than 4 lb.

Fishing on South Uist is in the hands of the South Uist Estate and managed on their behalf by Captain John Kennedy, Lochboisdale Hotel. Angling guests wishing to fish South Uist waters are expected to stay at Lochboisdale; although from time to time places are also available in private fishing parties based at Grogarry Lodge, a superb Victorian shooting lodge at the north end of the island.

Few other places in Scotland offer such a range of outstanding sport; and South Uist is perhaps one of the world's last remaining really great fishing locations, where anglers will find absolute peace and quiet – and tremendous sport.

12. Inverness-shire

The Beauly and Glass

LOCATION: Ordnance Survey Landranger Series, 1: 50,000. 25, Glen Carron and 26, Inverness.

GRID REFERENCES: Sheet 25, Loch Monar, 140405; Loch Affric, 155223; Loch Beinn a' Mheadhoin, 235246. **Sheet 26**, Glass and Farrar confluence, 408398; Cannich, 340314; Eskdale House, 467411; Lovat Waters, 517446; Beauly Firth, 600475.

SEASON: Salmon – February 11–October 15, with the best time in autumn. Trout – April 1–September 30, with the prime time during early summer.

FLIES: Salmon – Garry Dog, Silver Stoat's Tail, Willie Gunn, Munro Killer, General practitioner. Trout – Peter Ross, Soldier Palmer, Dunkeld, Silver Butcher, Hairy Mary.

COSTS: A day ticket will cost from £8.25 up to £40 for salmon fishing. Trout permits are available from £3 per rod per day.

PERMISSION: Lovat Estate: Lovat Estate Office, Beauly, Inverness-shire (Tel: 0463–782205).
Beauly, Glass, and Trout Lochs: Glen Affric Hotel, Cannich, Inverness-shire (Tel: 04565–214).

THE BEAULY DRAWS its water from the North-west Highlands, north of the Great Glen. Its huge catchment area drains deep, dark lochs and gathers in narrow tumbling burns, little lochans and peaty rivers. It enters the North Sea after washing out of its own wide firth into the Moray Firth.

The whole Beauly system has been harnessed by the North of Scotland Hydro-electric Board. It is a maze of dams, power-stations and by-pass tunnels. Salmon-ladders have been incorporated in some dams and river levels are controlled. One benefit is that Beauly is fishable most of the time.

The two rivers that meet to form the Beauly proper are the Farrar and Glass.

The Farrar begins life below the dam at Loch Monar, fed by burns from the surrounding empty mountains. Water is released to flow east and take in other tributaries. The main one, Uisge Misgeach, has a power-station on it. Migratory fish are denied access to Monar Loch by the huge dam at its eastern end and consequently have to spawn elsewhere.

The headwater of the Glass are split between the Affric and the Cannich. The Affric tumbles from Bheinn Fhada (1,032 m) through ancient Caledonian Affric Forest into beautiful, remote

Loch Affric, which spills over into Loch Beinn a'
Mheadhoin. Trout in these water average 12 oz,
and baskets of six or more are common.

Salmon running the Affric are heading for
spawning grounds in the river above Loch Affric.
Unwary brown-trout anglers may end up playing
a salmon!

Much of Loch Beinn a' Mheadhoin is
surrounded by trees. The Affric flows from the
dam at the eastern end of the loch, down through
a steep, wooded gorge, over Dog Falls and Badger
Falls. Its cascading waters are swollen by Abhainn
Deabhag Burn just below the second falls, and
then, below this meeting, is another dam at
Fasnakyle. This, coupled with the dam on the
Cannich at Loch Mullardoch, controls the flow
down Strath Glass.

INSURMOUNTABLE FALLS

The Cannich is inaccessible to salmon because
of insurmountable falls, but lochs on its dammed
headwaters are excellent for brown-trout fishing.
It is at the conference of the Affric and Cannich,
just beyond the village of Cannich, that the Glass
proper is formed to weave its way to meet the
Farrar, near Struy village, and to form the Beauly.

Beauly fishing is ought-after, but when you
hear of salmon catches exceeding 40 in one day,
that is little wonder. There are two dams on the
Beauly, one at Aigas, the other at Kilmorack. Fish
are counted at them and an average of 7,000 pass
through each year.

Early in 1990, Simon Fraser, of Lovat Estates,
put seven beats of Beauly on the market. The
asking price was £12 million.

Beats of the Beauly from the Glass and Farrar
junction to the estuary are Farrar Junction, Aigas

R IVER BEAULY. Seven
beats of Beauly went
on the market in early
1990, the asking price
was twelve million
pounds. An average of
seven thousand fish are
counted through the two
dams on the river each
year.

Eskadale and Beaufort Castle. Each fishes four
rods at a time, and in prime months at least five
fish a day may be caught.

The Beaufort Castle, or Lovat Estate, beats
include Falls, Home and Downie. It was from the
last that J Szarkiewicz took a 19 lb salmon from
Greenbank Pool in 1989. On Falls, Glide Pool can
always be relied on to produce fish, Castle Pool

and Charlie's have both given salmon of more
than 12 lb.

Most of the Beauly sea-trout spawn below
Kilmorack Dam, and the best time to fish for time
is in July. They average about 1½ lb.

The lower reaches of the Beauly are beautiful,
with gentle woods and fields dotted with grazing
cattle and sheep. Catching a salmon is almost a bonus.

The Ness and Loch Ness

LOCATION: Ordnance Survey Landranger Series, 1: 50,000. 34, Fort Augustus, and 26, Inverness.

GRID REFERENCE: Sheet 34, Fort Augustus, 381095. **Sheet 26**, Foyers, 495219; Urquhart Castle, 531286; Loch Ness, 580340; Dochfour, House, 604392; Inverness Town Water, 665442.

SEASONS: Salmon January 15–October 15, with August, September and October best. Trout March 15–October 6, with best fishing in May, June, July and August.

FLIES: Salmon Black Stoat, Silver Stoat, Thunder Stoat, Jeannie, Munro Killer. Trout Peter Ross, Black Pennell, Soldier Palmer, Dunkeld, Invicta, Hairy Mary, March Brown.

COSTS: A day on Loch Ness for two rods, with boat and gillie, will cost £35. On the Town Water, expect to pay between £5 and £10 per rod per day.

PERMISSION: Ness: Inverness Angling Club, J Graham, 71 Castle Street, Inverness (Tel: 0463–233178).
Ness: Dochfour Estate Office, Dochgarroch, Inverness (Tel: 046386–218).
Loch Ness: Foyers Hotel, Foyers, Inverness-shire (Tel: 04563–216).
Loch Ness: Glenmoriston Estate Office, Invermoriston by Inverness (Tel: 0320–51202).
Loch Ness: Inchnacardoch Lodge Hotel, Fort Augustus, Inverness-shire (Tel: 0320–6258).
Loch Ness: Cluanie Inn, Glenmoriston, Inverness-shire (Tel: 0320–40238).

THE NESS IS a short salmon and sea-trout river connecting mighty Loch Ness with the Moray Firth. Following its course are the last reaches of the Caledonian Canal, which follows the Highland Fault Line up The Great Glen, joining west coast with east.

The canal, which makes use of the lochs as well as artificial cuts, was opened in October, 1822. Many hardy Highland men were employed in its construction, much needed work following their discharge from the army after the Napoleonic Wars. The cost of this short-cut from the Atlantic to the North Sea was £1,300,000. A cruise along the canal is the best way to view the glen, but remember to look in on the Moriston, Garry, Oich, Spean and Lochy on the way.

Salmon and sea-trout catches number several hundred fish each year. Inverness Town Water had its finest season for many years in 1988, with 539 salmon and grilse and 426 sea-trout taken. Prime months for salmon fishing are September and October, but the best runs of sea-trout occur in late June and July. Sea-trout may not be fished for on Inverness AC waters until May 1.

'MONSTER' SIGHTINGS

Some beats on the Ness are private and can figure only in dreams. But, if you can, try fishing Little Isle, General's Well, Weir Pool, MacIntyre or Mill Stream. In September, 1989, Raymond Black took a 19 lb salmon from Weir Pool, which sometimes yields three salmon a day. General's Well is an excellent summer pool, and can be

relied on to give good sport. On Dochfour, which begins where Loch Ness ends, Raymond Breau caught a 25 lb salmon from Berry's Wall in July, 1988.

Loch Ness is home of 'The Monster'. If you believe in it, the best place to have a possible sighting is from the promontory on which stand the grey ruins of Castle Urquhart, between Foyers and Invermoriston. Fortified buildings have stood here since before historical records began. The last owners were Chiefs of Clan Grant. Decay set in after the Castle was blown up in 1689 by Government troops in an attempt to deter early Jacobite supporters.

FIGHTING FISH

Returning salmon and sea-trout seem to swim up the south-east shore of the loch, venturing across the water only when opposite their native river. Around 500 salmon are taken each year over the 24-mile length of Ness with late summer and autumn best for salmon and July and August for sea-trout. Salmon average approaching 10 lb with heavier fish taken regularly, especially off the 'estuaries' of the incoming rivers. Sea-trout usually weigh around 1 lb 8 oz.

The loch is divided into beats, all of which yield wonderful, fighting brown trout and ferox. Trout of 2 lb can be caught along the loch margins, with a multitude of bays and inlets from which to choose. Trolling is not allowed, so anglers have to be extra skilful, and lucky, to lure a ferox. In places, the Loch plunges to more than

600 ft deep.

Fishing is most productive from a boat, and it is wise always to employ a gillie. If you decide to handle your own boat, then beware of the strong winds which can sometimes whip up the Great Glen and turn the loch's surface into a white-waved cauldron. Head for home at the first sign of bad weather. The fish will always be there tomorrow.

The largest salmon ever taken from Loch Ness was a 55 pounder, a true 'monster'. Excellent advice, boat-hire and gillies are available from Foyers Hotel or Killianan Fishing at Portclair.

The Moriston

LOCATION: Ordnance Survey Landranger Series, 1: 50,000. Sheet 34, Fort Augustus.

GRID REFERENCES: Loch Cluanie, 140095; Loch Loyne, 155046; Loyne and Moriston confluence, 228114; Dundreggan, 322143; Invermoriston, 420165; Moriston estuary, 428162.

SEASONS: Salmon – January 15–September 30, with best sport from July until the close. Trout – March 15–September 30, with May and June best.

FLIES: Salmon Silver Stoat, Blue Charm, Garry Dog, Munro Killer, Willie Gunn. Trout – Peter Ross, Grouse and Claret, Teal and Silver, Black Pennell, Bloody Butcher.

COSTS: A day's salmon fishing on Moriston will cost from £6–£25 per rod per day according to the time of season.

PERMISSION: Moriston: Glenmoriston Estate Office, Glenmoriston, Inverness-shire (Tel: 0320–51202).
Loch Loyne: Tomdoun Hotel, Tomdoun, Invergarry, Inverness-shire (Tel: 08092–218).
Loch Loyne: Cluanie Inn, Glenmoriston, Inverness-shire (Tel: 0320–40238).
Loch Cluanie: Dochfour Estate Office, Dochgarroch, Inverness (Tel: 046386–218).

THE MORISTON FLOWS 16 miles from dammed Loch Cluanie to deep, forbidding Loch Ness. Cluanie plunges to depths of more than 180 ft and is nearly eight miles long. It holds good stocks of native brown trout.

The loch lies amid beautiful, rugged mountains where the wind forever sings. Its trout average 1 lb, with boat fishing producing best results, especially around the islands. Good baskets may be had also from the shallower margins.

From Cluanie, the Moriston flows east along Glen Moriston, its sides speckled with ash-white remains of the ancient Caledonian Forest. The old 'Road to the Isles' follows the course of the river.

It was in this timeless glen that Bonnie Prince Charlie met with the 'Seven men of Glen Moriston'. They had fled here after the Battle of Culloden, and protected and hid him from searching Hanoverian troops. When he finally parted from them, on August 12, 1746, he rewarded them with 24 guineas to be divided equally. Betrayal would have fetched them £30,000.

Two miles from Loch Cluanie, the Moriston is met by the Loyne, spilling from dammed Loch Loyne. The combined waters tumble on to gather in the Doe, just beyond Ceannacroc Bridge.

On the Moriston's next stretch, to Dundreggan Reservoir, stands MacKenzie's Cairn. Roderick Mackenzie was son of an Edinburgh jeweller and an ardent Jacobite supporter. He eventually became personal guard to Bonnie Prince Charlie, for whom he gave his life when he was captured and beheaded by Hanoverian troops. He resembled his beloved prince in looks and mannerisms, and his final words were that they had at last killed Prince Charlie. The resulting confusion gained valuable time for the Prince, who eventually escaped to France.

Dundreggan Reservoir, created by the North of Scotland Hydro Board, has a fish-pass in its dam, and fish are thus able to gain access to the Moriston's upper reaches. The western area of this stocked loch produces the best baskets of fish. Trout average 1 lb, and in summer more than 10 fish may be caught in an evenings fishing.

The best salmon fishings lie below Dundreggan, where most fish are caught by spinning. They average around 11 lb, and more than 230 are taken each season. Fish of 20–30 lb are not uncommon, and the heaviest Moriston salmon weighed 55 lb. It's well worth searching for another.

The Garry

LOCATION: Ordnance Survey Landranger Series, 1: 50,000. Sheets 33, Loch Alsh and Glen Shiel, and 34, Fort Augustus.

GRID REFERENCES: Sheet 33, Loch Quoich, 010020. **Sheet 34**, Loch Poulary, 125014; Tomdoun Hotel, 157011; Loch Inchlaggan, 185013; Loch Garry, 240025; Invergarry, 303010; Loch Oich, 325014.

SEASONS: Salmon – March 15–October 6, with spring the best time. Trout – March 15–October 6, with the best fishing in early summer.

FLIES: Salmon – Munro Killer, Garry Dog, Blue Charm, Hairy Mary, General Practitioner, Jeannie. Trout – Peter Ross, Grouse and Claret, Silver Butcher, Bloody Butcher, Dunkeld, Black Spider.

COSTS: A day's salmon fishing on the Garry will cost from £17–£35 a day, depending on time of season. Trout fishing on the lochs will be around £3 per day. A boat costs about £8 per day, including the fishing.

PERMISSION: Garry and Loch Oich: Rod and Gun Shop, Station Square, Fort William, Inverness-shire (Tel: 0397–2656).
Garry: Mr R B Scott, Post Office, Invergarry, Inverness-shire (Tel: 08093–201).
Garry and Lochs Garry, Poulary, Inchlagan and Quoich: Tomdoun Hotel, Tomdoun, Invergarry, Inverness-shire (Tel: 08092–218).
Loch Garry and Loch Inchlaggan: Garry Gualach Adventure Centre, Invergarry, Inverness-shire (Tel: 08092–230).

FROM INVERMORISTON AND the Moriston's estuary into Loch Ness, the lochside road takes you south-west down the Great Glen to Invergarry, standing guard at the eastern entrance to beautiful Glen Garry and overlooking the estuary of its river.

The Inverness-shire Garry, not to be confused with the Perthshire Garry, collects its waters from the western mountains, almost overlooking Loch Hourn and Loch Nevis on the west coast. They gather in Loch Quoich and flow on through Loch Poulary to Loch Inchleggan and Loch Garry. The flow is controlled at dams at the eastern ends of Loch Quoich and Loch Garry, from where the river flows to its estuary in Loch Oich, joined by the River Oich to the western end of Loch Ness.

Brown-trout fishing in wild and desolate, wind-swept Glen Garry is challenging. It is by fly only, and trout run from 12 oz–1 lb, but in deeper Quoich and Garry are predatory ferox which grow to unknown weights.

Quoich, the topmost loch on the Garry system, drains many Munro mountains, the most magnificent of them Sgurr na Ciche (1,040 m), 'Peak of Corries'. On calm summer days its ravaged, barely covered slopes are mirrored in the loch's still waters. Salmon and sea-trout are denied access to Quoich by the dam, but they do spawn in the river and in Kingie Burn, which meets with Garry at Kingie Pool, about a mile west of Loch Poulary.

In 1978 J A F Jackson landed a 19 lb 9¼ oz trout, and more recent seasons have seen many of

LOCH GARRY. This could be the place to catch that brown trout for the glass-case. Even if you don't, you should at least have one fine 14 oz specimen; and few places are as beautiful to fish.

more than 10 lb taken. This really could be the place to get one for the glass-case. The loch's wealth of stony bays are begging to be fished. It is best to book a boat with outboard motor to get about. Being a deep loch, Quoich can appear dour at times; catching her fish is definitely a challenge.

MAN-MADE BEAUTY

From here, the Garry meanders down the glen, broadening at the foot of Drum na h-Achlasie (137 m) to form Loch Poulary. This shallow loch is man-made, the effect of the river backing-up after being dammed. During summer it can become quite weedy. The best fishing is from a boat along the original course of the river.

From Poulary, Garry meanders past Tomdoun Hotel, an excellent base for a fishing holiday. The hotel has rights to many waters in the surrounding area, and first-class advice can be had for the asking.

The Garry broadens again into Loch Inchlaggan, another man-made loch. Here, too, the best sport is from a boat, following the course of the old river before Inchlaggan spills directly into Loch Garry at Torr na Carraidh.

Loch Garry is one of Scotland's most beautiful lochs. In spring wild snow-sprinkled mountains rise high above creeping mists. Later, dark conifer plantations huddled close to the shores are interspersed with silver birth and blazing rowan. Its waters hold brown trout of uncommon size. At its deepest, the loch plunges to 150 ft. In 1965 K J Grant landed a ferox of 19 lb 2oz to a Black Pennell! Occasional salmon and sea-trout are taken on the loch, but they are not plentiful.

From Loch Garry the river winds its way to Invergarry and into Loch Oich, in the Great Glen. Each season salmon are trapped and stripped of their ova and milt at a hatchery here, and the resultant fry are planted out in the main river and Kingie Burn.

The dam on Loch Garry has a fish-counter in its fish-pass, and more than 200 salmon are counted through each year. The best fishing months are late April, May and June, and they are priced accordingly. Salmon average 7 lb and sea-trout $1\frac{1}{2}$ lb.

Glen Garry offers all that an angler could wish for – first-class fishing at value-for-money costs in a beautiful and remote setting.

The Lochy, Spean and Roy

LOCATION: Ordnance Survey Landranger Series, 1: 50,000. 34, Fort Augustus, and 41, Ben Nevis.

GRID REFERENCES: Sheet 34, Loch Lochy, 108747; Loch Arkaig, 125905; Loch Laggan, 475855; Glen Spean, 290805; Glen Roy, 313894; Roy and Spean confluence, 272806; Bridge of Mucomuir, 184839; Lochy and Loy confluence, 152816; **Sheet 41**, Lochy, 136792; Nevis estuary, 108747; Loch Linnhe, 085740.

SEASONS: Salmon – May 1–September 30, with the best sport in autumn. Trout – April 1–September 30, with early summer best.

FLIES: Salmon – Willie Gunn, Munroe Killer, Garry Dog, Jeannie, Silver Stoat, Hairy Mary. Trout – Black Pennell, Peter Ross, Invicta, Cinnamon and Gold, Silver Butcher, Dunkeld.

COSTS: A week's salmon fishing on the Lochy will cost £150 per rod. The river beats fish only two rods at a time. A day on Spean or Roy will cost up to £15 per rod, depending on time of season.

PERMISSION: Lochy, Nevis, Spean and Roy: Rod and Gun Shop, Fort William, Inverness-shire (Tel: 0397–2656). **Spean:** Spean Bridge Hotel, Spean Bridge, Inverness-shire (tel: 039781–250). **Loch Lochy:** No permission needed. **Loch Arkaig:** Locheil Estate Fishings, West Highland Estate Office, 33 High Street, Fort William, Inverness-shire (Tel: 0397–2433).

LEAVING GLEN GARRY, the A82 road takes you past a monument. It commemorates the swift course of feudal justice. On top of the monument are seven stone heads which, according to legend, represent seven brothers, kinsmen of Chief Keppoch and his brother. The seven brothers killed them and stole their lands. The remainder of Keppoch Clan were not happy about this, so they beheaded the lot and washed their heads in a nearby well. The seven heads were then presented to the Chief of Glengarry in 1663, but it was not until 1812 that the monument was erected by the last Chief MacDonnel of Glengarry.

Beyond the monument, the road crosses the Caledonian Canal and continues down the Great Glen along the shore of Loch Lochy, connected to the sea by the Rivery Lochy.

Rushing in from the east, to meet with the Lochy, are the Spean and Roy. Spean was harnessed many years ago by the British Aluminium Company, and the flow is poor compared to what it was. But as the river hurries down Glen Spean from Loch Laggan, so it takes in sparkling feeder burns until, passing through steep, rocky gorges and past banks of conifers, silver birch and rowan, it reaches Roybridge and the River Roy, charging off Beinn Iaruinn, Carn Dearg and far-off Braeroy Forest.

It is in the Roy that most sea-trout and salmon spawn. Its course is narrow and rocky, and its source is close to Loch Spey, source of that famous river. Having only two small feeder lochs, Roy can become a mere trickle in summer.

The best fishing on the Spean is from Roy Junction down to the meeting with the Lochy. Hundreds of sea-trout are taken each year for an average of 1½ lb. A number of salmon are also landed, and they average 8 lb, though each season sees fish of more than 20 lb caught.

The Spean sweeps into the Lochy at Bridge of Mucomir. The Lochy is the last water link along the Great Glen between east and west coasts. Its course is straight and swift, through deep and inviting stony pools and over bubbling rapids until, after eight miles, it spills into Loch Linnhe's salt-water at Fort William. This town is a bustling tourist centre and a perfect base for a fishing holiday.

Loch Lochy which the Lochy drains, can be fished for free. Its deep waters hide brown trout to more than 5 lb, but they have to be worked for, and are best tackled from a boat.

FOR THE GLASS CASE

Draining into Loch Lochy from the west is Loch Arkaig, which yields good baskets of 10 oz brown trout. Occasional sea-trout and salmon are also caught, and the best places to fish are where feeder burns splash into the loch. Trolling could produce that glass-case specimen.

The Lochy itself has more than 45 pools. Many look shallow, but don't be deceived. Wade with care. The banks are gentle pastureland spiked with windbreaks of Scots pine and silver birch.

The next tributary to flow into the Lochy is the Loy. It is dammed, but has a fish-pass and excellent spawning grounds for salmon which, with sea-trout, move upstream from late spring.

LOCH LOCHY. This is the last loch in the Great Glen, linking east to west. Although fishing is free the brown trout have to be worked for. Anglers may be rewarded though for their efforts with one of 5 lb.

public and accounts for around 450 fish each
One of the lower beats, Beat 7, is available to the
season. The best times to fish are in wet summer
months, September and October.

More than 600 salmon and 1,500 sea-trout are
taken annually from the length of Lochy. It is a
beautiful river to fish, set amid the wildest
Scottish mountains, with Ben Nevis's lofty
summit glowering over all.

Just as the Lochy flows into Loch Linnhe, it is
swollen by the Nevis. This river thunders down
Glen Nevis, gathering in white waters from
surrounding peaks. Snow on these high ridges
keeps the Nevis at adequate levels for most of the
season. Its sea-trout fishing can be spectacular,
with fish averaging just over 1 lb. Salmon are also
caught, but not as frequently as sea-trout. They
weigh usually from 5–6 lb, with heavier fish taken
in the autumn.

Remember, though, that when you come to
this area to fish, you will not be alone. Thousands
of tourists come to do battle with the mountains
every summer.

RIVER SPEAN. This
first class sea-trout
water also holds salmon
and brown trout. It
connects the famous
River Lochy with the
River Roy, the place
where most returning
salmon go to spawn.

Loch Shiel and Loch Eilt

LOCATION: Ordnance Survey Landranger Series, 1: 50,000. Sheet 40, Loch Shiel.

GRID REFERENCES: Loch Ailort, 768824; Loch Eilt, 805825; Loch Shiel, 830735.

SEASONS: Salmon – February 11–October 31 on Ailort Loch Shiel fishing does not begin until April. Trout – April 1–September 30.

FLIES: Salmon – Munro Killer, Hairy Mary, Silver Stoat's Tail, Garry Dog, Jeannie. Trout – Black Pennell, Peter Ross, Grouse and Claret, various Butchers.

COSTS: A day's fishing will be in the region of £10, including the use of a boat with outboard motor.

PERMISSION: Loch Shiel: Glenfinnan House Hotel, Glenfinnan, Inverness-shire (Tel: 039783–235).
Loch Shiel: Stage House Inn: Glenfinnan, Inverness-shire (Tel: 039783–246).
loch Shiel: D Macaulay, Dalilea Farm, Acharacle, Argyll (Tel: 096785–253).
Ailort and Loch Eilt: Lochailort Inn, Lochailort, Inverness-shire (Tel: 06877–208).

TRAVELLING WEST FROM Fort William on the A830, you come to the quiet village of Glenfinnan. Stretching south, behind the village, is Loch Shiel.

It was on the shores of Loch Shiel, on August, 19, 1745, that the Standard was raised to mark the beginning of the 1745 Jacobite uprising. At the northern end of the loch stands a commemorative monument, erected in 1815 by Alexander MacDonald of Glenaladale, a descendant of the MacDonalds who had supported the uprising.

In the background, over the River Finna, is Britain's first ferro-concrete railway viaduct. It was built in 1906 and is well in keeping with the surrounding summits of rugged, windswept Sgurr Thuilm (964 m), Sgurr nan Coireach (956 m) and Sgurr on Utha (796 m). At the southern end of the loch is famous St Finnan's Isle, Eilean Fhionain, ancient burial ground of MacDonalds and home of St Finnan's Bell, which used to be carried at the front of funeral processions.

One famous visitor to Loch Shiel's shores was Queen Victoria. I often wonder if Bonnie Prince Charlie's ghost knew of her Stuart connections. If so, did he finally rest in peace, safe with the knowledge that a descendant of the Stewarts was once more on the throne?

The Shiel tumbles out of the western end of the loch into its sea-loch, Loch Moidart. Access for salmon and sea-trout is easy, and seals occasionally take advantage of this fact. The best runs of sea-trout are in July. Salmon enter the loch

RIVER SHIEL. Storm clouds are gathering over the surrounding mountains. Shiel's crystal clear waters are best fished when a slight breeze ruffles the surface or after heavy rainfall. These conditions are necessary when angling for shy sea-trout.

LOCH SHIEL. It is not only a fisherman's paradise but a seal's idea of heaven too, occasional grey bodies are spotted swimming in the loch. Although a rival, who can object to sharing the fish with them?

from June, with autumn the most productive time.

Loch Shiel has some delightful sand and gravel bays, excellent spawning grounds. The southern part of the loch is shallow, but further north it plunges to dark depths of more than 350 ft. The best fishing is by boat in the bays and shallower areas.

The loch also carries a stock of fine brown trout, with fish of more than 2 lb not uncommon. A more likely basket for a day's fishing will be of nice 12 oz trout.

Shiel is one of Scotland's most beautiful lochs. Mountains soar all around their slopes clothed with deer grass and heather. Conifers cover parts of the shore, casting long shadows over the rippled water. It is a fisherman's paradise.

MIDSUMMER NIGHTS

The River Shiel's clear waters provide first-class sea-trout fishing, especially in pools such as Grassy Point, Boat, Parapet, Garrison and Sea. Its course has been much altered by man to create more pools and lies. Fishing is best when a wind ruffles the crystal water or after heavy rain on the mountains.

Leaving Glenfinnan, the A830 soon takes you to the shores of Loch Eilt. This loch is dammed at the western end, and fish ascending the River Ailort have to wait for heavy rain or an artificial freshet before they can gain access to the loch. Salmon and sea-trout spawn in the feeder burns.

Sea-trout enter the River Ailort from Loch Ailort, its sea-loch, in July, when sport in the river can be fast and furious. Good pools are Falls, McPherson's, Monument, Lord Elgin's and New Bridge. The best salmon fishing is in autumn.

Eilt's brown trout average 1 lb, but bigger fish are not uncommon. The loch's margins can give good results, as can the narrower, western reaches.

Eilt, again, is surrounded by craggy mountains, their grass and heather slopes scattered with silver birch and rowan. It is an enchanted loch, a perfect place to spend a midsummer night in search of sea-trout.

LOCH EILT offers excellent sport amongst magnificent scenery. Hire a boat, with outboard, and begin your search around loch margins and in the western end. A gentle breeze and dull skies, you can't fail.

13. Caithness

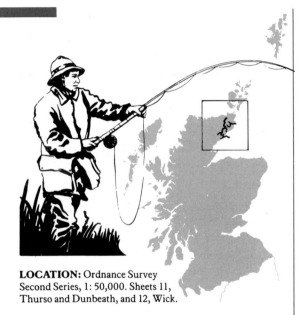

LOCATION: Ordnance Survey Second Series, 1: 50,000. Sheets 11, Thurso and Dunbeath, and 12, Wick.

GRID REFERENCES: Sheet 11, Ulbster Arms Hotel and Thurso River, 129595; Falls Pool, Forss River, 037687; **Sheet 12, Wick River at Bilbster Mains, 283535; Loch of Wester, 325592; Loch Watten, 230560; Loch St John's, 225720; Loch Heilen, 255685.**

SEASONS: Salmon – January 11–October 10; Forss and Wick open on February 11. Best month, September. Trout – The season starts on March 15; but Watten and Heilen do not open until May 1. Best months, June and September.

FLIES: Salmon – Green Highlander, Garry Dog, Thunder and Lightning, Hairy Mary, General Practitioner, Shrimp Fly, Munro Killer, Black Doctor, Waddingtons. Sea-trout and brown trout – Ke-He, Black Pennell, Soldier Palmer, Invicta, Black Zulu, Blue Zulu, Greenwell's Glory, March Brown, Woodcock and Hare-lug, Grouse and Claret, Silver Butcher, Alexandra, Dunkeld, Silver Invicta.

COSTS: Salmon fishing, when available, costs £20–£35 per rod per day on the Thurso and Forss, but considerably less on the Wick River. A boat with outboard motor and fuel, with two rods fishing, costs around £18 per day.

PERMISSION: Thurso River: Ulbster Arms Hotel, Halkirk, Caithness (Tel: 084783 206).
Forss River: Salar Management Services Ltd, Lochloy House, Nairn (Tel: 0667 55355).
Wick River: Hugo Ross, Breadalbane Terrace, Wick, Caithness (Tel: 0955 4200).
Loch Wester: A Dunnet, Auchorn Farm, Lyth, by Wick, Caithness (Tel: 095583-208).
Loch Watten: D Gunn, Watten Lodge, Watten, Caithness (Tel: 095582 217).
Loch St John's: Northern Sands Hotel, Dunnet, Caithness (Tel: 084785 270).
Loch Heilen: H Pottinger, Greenland Mains, Castletown, Caithness (Tel: 084782-210).

CAITHNESS IS MAINLAND Britain's most northerly county; a magnificent landscape, blanketed by beautiful peat moorlands which sparkle silver and blue with trout-filled lochs.

Dramatic mountains line the southern horizon: the Scarabens and Morven. Highland rivers, bright with Atlantic salmon, cascade seawards. The air is champagne-fresh and skies seem endless. It's a wonderful, peaceful world, where angling dreams came true.

But in recent years, Caithness has been the centre of controversy between commercial tree-planters and conservationists, arguing over the fate of the Flow Country; vast, magnificent moorlands which stretch from the slopes of Ben Loyal in the west to wave-lashed eastern cliffs guarding Caithness from the cold fury of the North Sea.

More than 100,000 acres of irreplaceable moorland have been ploughed and planted with foreign species of confier, destroying a habitat that has lain virtually undisturbed for 7,000 years.

Sitka spruce and lodge-pole pine march in their millions across once empty hills; electrified fences and locked gates enclose an area where anglers and naturalists used to walk freely.

Recently, a measure of agreement has been reached to curtail further damage to the Flow Country by unrestricted forestry, and the Highland Regional Council has designated areas which it deems undesirable for planting. Sadly, these efforts have come much too late to save the

RIVER THURSO.
There are fourteen
beats on this river and
upwards of 1,000 salmon
are taken each season.
This river used to be one
of the best spring waters
to be on, but recent
seasons have seen
autumn months more
productive.

LOCH HEILEN. Although a hard loch to fish the shallow waters can give rewards well worth the effort as this 4 lb 8 oz wild brown trout proves. Fish of under 2 lb should be returned . . . .

Above
LOCH ARKAIG. The
new day dawns over
the water and in its
stillness the rings of
rising trout can be seen.
A sight to gladden the
anglers heart. This loch
spills into Loch Lochy
and is also home to
occasional sea-trout and
salmon.

Left
LOCH WATTEN. An
evening catch for
two anglers. The trout in
these waters are a
mixture of native brown
trout and a Loch Leven
strain that was intro-
duced in the 1920s. The
result is a loch full of
hard fighting fish.

LOCH KATRINE. M[ost]
beautiful of all the
Trossach Lochs. Her
deep waters are home [to]
hard fighting wild bro[wn]
trout. Although it can [be]
a dour loch it is well
worth the effort to cat[ch]
them.

heart of the Flows, since most of the areas now identified as being unsuitable have already been planted.

The spectre of nuclear waste also threatens Caithness. Nirex, the Government's nuclear-waste disposal agency seems determined to site Europe's nuclear waste dump in Caithness, regardless of the results of a recent referendum, in which 57 per cent of those voting said 'No!' to Nirex.

AUTUMN GLORY

Nevertheless, in spite of the impact of tax-avoidance, blanket forestry and the prospect of nuclear waste disposal, Caithness still offers splendid opportunities for gamefishing. But my advice would be to make your visit soon, before the county becomes an international radioactive nuclear-waste dumping ground; and while some of the Flow Country is still left to be seen.

The Thurso is the county's pre-eminent salmon river. It was once regarded as one of the finest Scottish spring rivers; unfortunately, like so many other of Scotland's great rivers, spring runs seem to be a thing of the past, and the best sport now is invariably during autumn.

Thurso salmon average about 9 lb, and each season produces upwards of 1,000 fish, some of which weight more than 20 lb. Unfortunately, the Thurso is also one of the few remaining rivers in Scotland where estuary nets still operate. Were they removed, it is likely that the rods would have much better sport.

As it is, in drought conditions, such as prevailed during the long, hot, summer of 1989, thousands of salmon are scooped up by the nets as they wait for rain in Thurso Bay. In 1989 the rain

LOCH WATTEN. This shallow loch is home to wild brown trout of up to 3 lb. Fishing in the bays and around the island can produce some of the best baskets. Make sure you hire an outboard, as winds never blow in the anglers favour.

RIVER FORSS. One lucky angler who did his rain dance, and had his prayer answered fishes Falls Pool in the hope that his other wishes will be granted. The thundering white water throws up spray like steam from a boiling kettle.

didn't come until after the season had closed.

The Thurso rises on the slopes of Knockfin Heights (437 m), and is formed where the clear waters of Glutt Water and Rumsdale Water come together at Dalnagachan, hurrying them over the moorlands, past Dalnawillan, to Loch More. The other major tributary is Sleach Water, flowing east through the new plantations, from Lochan Dubh na Feithe Caoile, near Altnabreac.

The water level in the Thurso is controlled by a dam and sluices at Loch More, so reasonable fishing levels can be assured throughout the season unless the Loch becomes very low. The river is divided into 14 beats, each fishing to rods, who are expected to stay at the Ulbster Arms Hotel in Halkirk. The hotel has recently been completely refurbished and is very comfortable.

The Thurso is a delightful river to fish. Most of the beats can be tackled without much wading, and fly-only is the rule. A 13 ft double-handed salmon rod covers most eventualities. Gillies are available.

SPATE SPORT

A few miles west of Thurso, the delightful little Forss River can also give wonderful sport. The Forss flows out of Loch Shurrery, wending its way slowly north through low-lying, boggy country to reach the sea at Crosskirk Bay. It is very much a spate stream and really needs good water levels to give of its best.

The Forss was until recently a private river. Indeed, the Upper Forss still is private; but the lower river, which gives the best fishing, has been timeshared by Salar Properties Ltd. The company has removed all nets from the estuary and has thus ensured that returning salmon have easy access to the river in all but the lowest water. A hatchery has been established and a considerable amount of time and money has been spent on repairing the banks and re-instating damaged pools.

Lower Forss is divided into two beats, each fishing four rods, with anglers changing over at mid-day. Above Forss Falls, the river is a delightful stream, narrow, with deep holding pools and long glides.

Falls Pool is the most productive pool on the river, and each season it produces about 60 salmon, some of them more than 15 lb. Downstream from Falls Pool, the river slows and there the technique of backing-up is used.

Even in low water conditions, provided a good wind is blowing from either north or south, this part of the river can always produce fish, even in low water. In August, 1989, when the river was very low, one visiting angler, using dry fly, landed six salmon in a morning.

Day-lets are sometimes available on the Forss, as is the opportunity for a week's fishing, when owners cannot manage to come north. Accommodation is in a comfortable hotel close to the river, or anglers may chose to self-cater. One advantage of taking a let on the Forss is that, should water conditions be low, then five boats are available on the best Caithness brown trout lochs.

The Wick River is another productive salmon stream, and most seasons see 250–300 salmon landed. Fishing is managed by the Wick Angling Association and day and week tickets are readily available at modest cost.

Most Wick salmon are caught on bait, but several fine pools are suited to fly-fishing. The river has a reputation for large fish, with an average weight of 9 lb and the largest salmon of recent years, caught in 1979, weighing 22 lb 2 oz.

The river is sluggish, dropping only 10 ft over a distance of nine miles, but given a good level, it can be a superb stream. But in times of drought, the river almost disappears, and its a case of waiting for a spate.

For reasons best known to themselves, sea-trout avoid the Thurso, Forss and Wick rivers. But they don't avoid the Wester system, a few miles north of Wick along the A9 road towards John O'Groats. This classic sea-trout water consisting of a short river and a loch offers wonderful sport in September and October.

The distance from the sea to the loch is only half-a-mile, so sea-trout have easy access. A few salmon also run the river and are occasionally caught, but the main interest is in the hard-fighting sea-trout. They average 1 lb 8 oz, with fish of more than 5 lb caught most seasons.

FERTILE WATERS

Caithness is famous also for the quality of its wild brown-trout fishing, and its principal water, Loch Watten, is considered by many to be one of the finest trout fisheries in the whole of Scotland.

Watten lies in the central Caithness plain, surrounded by fertile farmlands and low hills. It is about three miles long by up to three-quarters of a mile wide, and can at times be very windy. Boats are readily available for hire, mostly moored at the east end of the loch, but an outboard motor, or a strong, fit young friend, is essential, as is a drogue to slow a drifting boat and hold it broadside to the wind.

Watten is a shallow water, averaging about 8 ft in depth, and being nowhere deeper than 20 ft. It is lime rich, boasting a pH of 7.8 and supports an abundance of food for trout. The fish grow rapidly, are perfectly shaped and pink-fleshed.

It is said that, during the 1920s, a number of riparian owners introduced a Loch Leven strain of fish to Watten. Certainly some of the fish, and particularly those caught at the eastern end of the loch, bear a striking resemblance to their more famous Kinross cousins; indeed, because they are so silver, many visiting anglers imagine they are sea-trout. The trout at the west end of the loch tend to be darker and more traditionally trout-like, but this is probably no more than the consequence of different feeding patterns and micro-habitat.

What is certain is that Loch Watten trout are of the highest quality and a delight to catch. They rise well to surface flies and may be caught all over the loch, with no one area being better than another.

Loch St John's, near Dunnet Head, is another famous Caithness trout loch, renowned for the size and quality of its fish. In recent years, St John's has been under the management of an improvement association, and a tremendous amount of work has been done to raise the quality of the fishing.

For some years, native fish have been reared in the association's hatchery and released into the loch at about 5 inches. This has temporarily reduced the overall average weight of fish, but in the long term, the associations stocking policy should return the loch to its former high status.

The most notorious Caithness loch, where you may fish all day without seeing even a fin, is Loch Heilen, a shallow, wind-swept 170 acres, close to the sea near Castletown. However, Heilen has some superb wild brown trout which are well worth the effort involved in caching them. Fish of more than 8 lb have been caught in recent years and trout of 3 lb and more are common. Anything of less than 2 lb should be returned.

Caithness used to be renowned for its hill-lochs, but, sadly, the mass-afforestation has so radically altered the character of many of these fine waters that few anglers now bother to fish them. It is alleged, too, that forestry ploughing has seriously damaged water-quality, and that stocks of fish will diminish as water becomes more acid. In the meantime many of these lochs do still fish well.

All brown trout fishing in Caithness is by fly only, other than on Loch Calder, where spinning and worm fishing is allowed. But there is no free fishing in Caithness, and anglers should always make sure that they obtain proper permission before fishing.

RIVER FORSS. It is interesting to compare this photograph with the previous one of Falls Pool on Forss. It gives a clear indication of how heavy rainfall can totally alter the character of the river.

14. The Trossachs, Lothians, Fife and Kinross

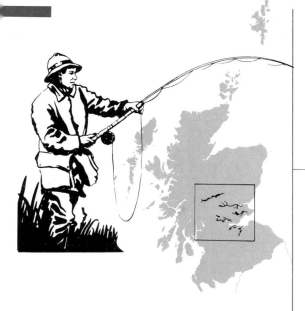

The Lothian Reservoirs Clubbiedean, Harperrigg and Gladhouse

LOCATION: Ordnance Survey Land Ranger 1:50,000. Sheets 66, Edinburgh, and 65, Falkirk and West Lothian.

GRID REFERENCES: Sheet 66, Clubbiedean Reservoir, 200667; Gladhouse Reservoir, 300535. **Sheet 65**, Harperrigg Reservoir, 095610.

SEASONS: Trout – April 1–September 30, with May and June best.

FLIES: Trout – Grouse and Claret, Black Pennell, Black Spider, March Brown, Silver Butcher, Bloody Butcher, Teal and Silver.

COSTS: A season ticket for any of the waters will cost around £25. Weekly and daily tickets are available at £1.70 and £9 respectively. Tweed for less than £10; some is as cheap as £1 for the entire season.

PERMISSION: Harperrigg, Gladhouse, Clubbiedean: Lothian Regional Council, Department of Water and Drainage, Comiston Spring, Buckstone Terrace, Edinburgh (Tel: 031445–4141).
Harperrigg: Department of Water and Drainage, Lomond House, Livingstone, West Lothian (Tel 0506–414004).

GLADHOUSE RESERVOIR. This water lies in the Moorfoot Hills. Over one thousand brown trout are taken each year. Best places to try are around shallower margins and by the islands. It is quite exposed so beware of the winds.

OF THE LOTHIAN reservoirs, the best on which to book a day are Gladhouse, Clubbiedean and Harperrig.

Clubbiedean, lying south-west of Edinburgh, near the bustling township of Currie, covers barely five hectares, yet it yields several hundred rainbow trout each season. Fishing is from three boats, with the exception of a couple of platforms built for disabled anglers. Trout average 1 lb and the Lothian Regional Council carries out annual restocking. But it is an accessible and popular water, book at least six weeks in advance to avoid disappointment.

Harperrig is set amid the desolate, wind-swept Pentland Hills. On its western shores lie the ruins of Cairns Castle, which once stood guard over the ancient Cauldstaneslap drove-road. The castle was built in 1440 by Sir William Crichton, Chancellor of Scotland.

WINTER GOOSE

Fishing on Harperrig is from both boat and bank, but bank anglers should pay heed to warnings about soft margins, quicksands and varying depths. Caution – and a ruffled surface – should yield at least one fish per rod per day. Trout of 3 lb are not uncommon, but most weigh from 12 oz to 1 lb. The loch is easily accessible, lying about 10 miles out of Edinburgh, close to the A70.

Over the Pentlands, eastwards into the Moorfoot Hills, lies Gladhouse Reservoir, the sight of which will gladden an angler's heart. Winter sees its waters packed with overwintering geese, and the noise is deafening. Gladhouse is part of a nature reserve and landing on its islands is forbidden, as is bank fishing. But eight boats cover its shallow waters, and around 1,200 brown trout are taken each season for an average weight of just under 1 lb. Trout of $2\frac{1}{2}$ lb and more are taken occasionally.

The best areas of Gladhouse are along the southern shoreline or in the shelter of North Island. Beware on windy days, for the surface can be whipped into a dangerous, boiling cauldron. And as on Clubbiedean, book well in advance. Patience could be rewarded with a heavier trout than the record nine-pounder.

Moving south into Border Country, many waters are worthy of attention. St Mary's Loch and Loch of the Lowes, part of the Tweed system, are perhaps two of the most beautiful.

Forth and Teith

LOCATION: Ordnance Survey Land Ranger 1:50,000. Sheets 57, Stirling and The Trossachs; 58, Perth and Kinross; and 65, Falkirk and West Lothian.

GRID REFERENCES: Sheet 57, Loch Ard, 465017; Teith Forth confluence, 769963; Callander, 628081.

SEASONS: Salmon – Feburary 1–October 31, with the best runs in autumn. Trout – March 15–October 6, with the best sport in summer.

FLIES: Salmon – Munro Killer, Black-and-gold, Stoat's Tail, Silver Stoat, Hairy Mary. Trout – Greenwell's Glory, Blue Dun, Black Spider, Dark Olive, Peter Ross, Mallard and Claret.

COSTS: Day tickets for Forth and Teith salmon fishing vary from £5–£20 according to the time of season.

PERMISSION: Forth and Allan: Messers D Crockart and Son, Tackle-dealers, 15 King Street, Stirling (Tel: 0786–73443).
Teith: J Bayne, 76 Main Street, Callander, Perthshire, (Tel: 0877–30218).
Loch Ard: Post Office, Kinlochard, Perthshire (Tel: 08777–284).
Loch Ard: Alskeith Hotel, Kinlochard, Perthshire (Tel: 08777–266).

TUMBLING FROM LOCH Ard, the Forth flows first through Milton village to gather in Duchary Water, snaking its way from the depths of dark and sprawling conifer plantations. From here, it meanders through the boggy ground of Gartrenich Moss Forest to swallow up Kelty Water and flow sluggishly on through fertile pastures. It is a slow, lazy river, often spilling over its banks after heavy rain to flood surrounding land.

Before reaching the Firth of Forth, the river is joined by the Teith, which drains Loch Venachar in the Trossachs. Venachar is now dammed and its waters used to quench the thirst of urban dwellers. But it is to the Teith that most salmon and sea-trout entering the Forth are heading to spawn. It is a friendly river to migratory fish, its current swift and its pools well formed.

Teith bubbles south to meet with the outflow of Loch Lubnaig, Keltie Water, Coillechat Burn, Annet Burn and Ardoch Burn, and the salmon's preference for it means that, of all the Forth system, it offers the best salmon fishing. More than 1,500 salmon are caught each season for an average weight of 9 lb. The main runs are in autumn, when salmon of more than 20 lb are taken. Sea-trout move into the river from early August. One of the best pools is Blue Bank. In August it can give a night to remember.

The Forth's next major tributary is Allan Water, which it meets on the outskirts of Stirling. Salmon, sea-trout and brown-trout fishing are all available on the Allan. Its river banks were once home to many factories, which coughed their waste into it. The cleaning-up of industrial activities, and the restocking of the feeder burns, is now promising a bright future for the river. Its

RIVER TEITH. This is the main tributary of the River Forth. It is to her waters that most salmon and sea-trout are heading. Access can be difficult in places due to the steeply wooded banks, but persevere, over 1,500 salmon are caught each season.

best salmon and sea-trout pools are on the lower reaches, but trout can be caught along its entire length.

After meandering through Stirling, the Forth runs a lazy course to its firth. Gone are the days when its was an open sewer, thanks to the excellent work and restocking carried out by the Forth District Salmon Fishery Board. Each year sees more salmon and sea-trout returning to spawn. The one sad note is that its upper lochs and feeders lie amid conifer plantation, with the consequent acidification and silting-up of spawning beds. For fish they are a death sentence.

The Trossachs Lochs

LOCATION: Ordnance Survey Land Ranger 1:50,000. Sheets 56, Loch Lomond, and 57, Stirling and the Trossachs.

GRID REFERENCES: Sheet 56, Loch Katrine, 425095. **Sheet 57**, Loch Katrine, 455100; Loch Achray, 515065; Loch Vencahar, 575055; Loch Lubnaig, 575137; Loch Voil, 503197.

SEASONS: Trout – March 15–October 6, with May, June and August the best months. Salmon – February 1–October 6, with the best sport in autumn.

FLIES: Trout – Grouse and Claret, Teal and Silver, Peter Ross, Invicta, Silver Butcher, March Brown, Greenwell's Glory. Salmon – Munro Killer, Garry Dog, Hairy Mary, Stoat's Tail.

COSTS: Brown trout fishing on the lochs costs from £1.50–£4 per day. Boat-hire is extra. Salmon fishing costs from around £3 per day.

PERMISSION: Loch Katrine: Strathclyde Regional Council, Water Department, 419 Balmore Road, Glasgow (Tel: 041336–5333).
Loch Venachar, Loch Lubnaig: J Bayne, Tackle-shop, Main Street, Callander, Perthshire (Tel 0877–30218).
Loch Voil: Ledcreigh Hotel, Balquidder, Strathyre, Perthshire (Tel: 08774–230).
Loch Achray: Forestry Commission, David Marshal Lodge, Aberfoyle, Perthshire.

MYSTERIOUS KATRINE, BEAUTIFUL Voil, shallow, wooded Lubnaig and Venachar, the pointed loch, are lochs of the Trossachs. Here, savage mountains soar skywards, craggy and inhospitable. It is Scotland's very heart, haunted, windswept, desolate.

Ben Ledi (879 m), Hill of the Gods is the highest, its rugged slopes soaring between Loch Venachar and Loch Lubnaig. Loch Voil is hidden in the north, behind Creag Mor (657 m), Ceann na Baintigherna (694 m) and Beinn an t-Sithein (570 m). Katrine is guarded by Ben Venue (727 m), hill of young cattle, and Beinn Bhreac (700 m), mountain of streams.

Many noted people have come to pay homage to the Trossachs, among them Wordsworth and his sister, Dorothy, Queen Victoria, and Sir Walter Scott. They doubtless saw the silver birch, purple heather, wild green sage and shining black whortleberries which grace the hills, but they didn't see the regimental conifer plantations which now blot the landscape, letting neither light nor wind kiss their pine-needle floors.

Fishing on the Trossachs lochs is mainly for wild brown trout, and for those who enjoy it, fishing on the Sabbath is permissible on all of them.

Loch Katrine plunges to depths of more than 400 ft and holds some trout. Fish of $2\frac{1}{2}$ lb and more are not uncommon, though most average about 12 oz. All fishing is from a boat, and by fly only. The best areas are in the shallower western and eastern extremes. It can be a hard, dour loch, but on the right day sport can be fast, furious and fun.

From the east end of Katrine, Achray Water flows into little Loch Achray. This shallow loch holds trout of 8–10 oz, and fishing is from the bank only. Achray is joined to Loch Venachar by Black Water.

SPARKLING WATERS

Venachar feeds the Teith, tributary of the Forth, and occasional sea-trout and salmon are taken. But it is the brown trout that offer most sport. Its western area offers a good chance of fish of 10 oz.

Tumbling from the north, also to feed the Teith, is Loch Lubnaig's outflow. This loch also yields occasional sea-trout and salmon, but again, brown trout provide the real sport. They average 10 oz and are caught mostly in the shallower northern end. Loch Lubnaig receives water from the Balvag, which drains Loch Voil.

Voil contains trout of around 10 oz, but bigger fish are not unknown, and its deep waters certainly shelter big ferox trout.

Come to fish the Trossachs lochs in June and July when the surrounding peaks are aglow with the colours of summer, and the water sparkles in the sun. The days may be too bright to fish, but evening could be another story.

The Earn

LOCATION: Ordnance Survey Land Ranger Series 1:50,000. Sheets 51, Loch Tay; 52, Aberfeldy and Glen Almond; and 58, Perth and Kinross.

GRID REFERENCES: Sheet 51, Loch Earn, 640235; Comrie,774221. **Sheet 52**, Crieff, 865217. **Sheet 58**, Aberuthven, 976154; Bridge of Earn, 132181.

SEASONS: Salmon – February 1–October 31, with autumn best. Trout – March 15–October 6, with early summer giving best sport.

FLIES: Salmon – Stoat's Tail, Munro Killer, Garry Dog, Blue Charm, General Practitioner. Trout – Grouse and Claret, Bloody Butcher, Blue Zulu, Peter Ross, Black Pennell, Teal and Silver, March Brown.

COSTS: Reasonable sport at a reasonable cost. You will pay up to £15 per day.

PERMISSION: Crieff: Crieff Angling Club, Secretary, Mr P McDougall, 2 Duchlage Terrace, Crieff, Perthshire (Tel: 0764–4539).
Crieff: W Cook & Sons, 19 High Street, Crieff, Perthshire (Tel 0764–2081).
Comrie: Royal Hotel, Comrie, Perthshire (Tel: 0764–3071).
Aberuthven: Aberuthven Farms Ltd, Aberuthven, Perthshire (Tel: 07646–2687).
Hilton: Bob Sime, Photographer, 57 Methven Street, Perth.
Hilton: Perth and District Anglers' Association, R Thom, 1 Schoonieburn Hill, Friarton, Perth.
Bridge of Earn: Managed Estates, 18 Maxwell Place, Stirling (Tel 0876-62519).

LOCH EARN. Sleepy dawn mists clear, a scorching day begins. Hardly a breath of wind ruffles the surface of this enchanting loch. Even though it is a popular loch for water sports it is often easy to find a quiet spot to do battle with rainbow and brown trout.

WEST OF LOCH Voil lies Loch Earn, and it is from here that the Earn begins her journey to mingle with the Tay as it spills in its firth. The river is noted for both sea-trout and salmon, as well as brown trout. In 1988, 1,309 sea-trout and 1,209 salmon were caught, with the salmon averaging around 10 lb and the sea-trout, 2 lb. Lady Mary's Walk, at Crieff, gave one angler a 7 lb 8 oz sea-trout in 1989. The best times are July and August for sea-trout, and autumn for salmon.

The Earn's course takes it along Strathearn, following part of the Highland Fault Line. To the east and south lie old red sandstones, and to the north and west, cold, hard quartzites and schists. Comrie, through which the river flows, is Britain's earthquake centre, and hydro dams in the area are built to withstand the occasional tremor.

Downstream from Comrie is Lochalane, a two-and-a-half-mile stretch which came on the market in 1989 for £570,000 – a sign perhaps of faith in the river's future.

Excellent work by the Earn Angling Improvement Association has led to the buying-out of all but two nets. Extensive stocking programmes are being followed with native fish, and a Protection Order to preserve the fishings has been granted.

As Earn is really a tributary of the Tay, it is worth hoping that some of the big Tay fish get lost and accidentally run the Earn. It's a thought worth bearing in mind as, in places, you struggle between the trees and down the river banks.

Loch Leven

LOCATION: Ordnance Survey Land Ranger Series, 1:50,000. Sheets 58, Perth and Kinross.

GRID REFERENCES: Sheet 58, Loch Leven 145015.

SEASONS: April 1–September 30, with June and July the best months.

FLIES: Trout – Traditional small double-hook flies do well. Black Pennell, Soldier Palmer, Invicta, Greenwell's Glory, March Brown, Woodcock, Grouse and Claret, Grouse and Green, Dunkeld, Hare-lug, Peter Ross, Hardies, Gold Butcher, Alexandra Butcher.

COSTS: Prices begin at £8. An evening session costs £20 in prime months, including boat-hire.

PERMISSION: The Pier, Kinross (Tel: 0577-63407).

AS YOU DRIVE south from the Earn, the M90 takes you by famous Loch Leven. Its waters lie amid the gentle plains of Kinross, and they are home to superb, hard-fighting brown trout which have been used to stock waters all over the world.

Forty 20 ft clinker-built boats are available on the six square miles of water, each fishing three rods. As most parts of Leven are shallow, trout can be caught all over. Fishing is fly-only.

The best times to fish Leven are in the evenings in June and July. The trout average about $1\frac{1}{4}$ lb, although many of more than 3 lb are taken. A recent season saw Francis Jarrett take one fish of 6 lb 6 oz. Around 20,000 fish are taken each year.

Trout in Leven often feed on the bottom, but this has not always been the case. Why the gradual change has occurred, no one knows, but anglers are now using sunk lines and English reservoir lures.

Perhaps the fish have shied away from the surface because of fishing pressure but fishermen and Leven go together. You will seldom, if ever, have the loch to yourself, but once you have landed your first Leven trout, you will be hooked on it for life.

Although Loch Leven Fisheries' hatchery is now used to stock the loch the number of trout taken each year is falling, and no one knows why. This trend has started only recently, and it is too soon to know whether fishing will improve, but the loch is still definitely worth a visit. All questions will be answered at The Pier, but telephone first to check whether boats are available.

Loch Rannoch and Loch Laidon

LOCATION: Ordnance Survey Land Ranger Series, 1:50,000. Sheets 51, Loch Tay, and 41, Ben Nevis.

GRID REFERENCES: Sheet 51, Loch Rannoch, 595575; Loch Laidon 563403. **Sheet 41**, Loch Laidon, 385545.

SEASONS: Trout – March 15–October 6, with the summer months offering superb sport.

FLIES: Trout – Wickham's Fancy, Silver Butcher, Teal and Silver, Greenwell's Glory, March Brown, Blue Zulu.

COSTS: Free to guests staying at Dunalastair Hotel. Casual visitors may obtain day tickets at £175. Boat-hire is £12 per day.

PERMISSION: Loch Rannoch and Loch Laidon: Moor of Rannoch Hotel, Rannoch Station, Perthshire (Tel: 08822–338).
Loch Rannoch: Dunalastair Hotel, Kinloch Rannoch, Perthshire (Tel 08822–323).
Loch Rannoch: Burnrannoch Hotel, Kinloch Rannoch, Perthshire (Tel 08822–367).
Loch Rannoch: Forestry Commission Campsite, Caire, Perthshire.
Loch Laidon: Moor of Rannoch Hotel, Rannoch Station, Perthshire (Tel: 08822–238).

L OCH RANNOCH CUTS a silver scar across Perthshire. In places its cold waters plunge to more than 300 ft deep, home to ferox trout of more than 20 lb. Climbing steeply away from the loch's eastern end is Scotland's most photographed Munro, Schiehallion (1,083 m). Translated, its name means 'Fairy Hill of the Caledonians'.

Much of Loch Rannoch's banks are now tightly packed with conifers though stands of birch still clothe some parts. The shallower margins of its western shores are the best fishing areas, and a day should yield three or four 12 oz trout. If you're in search of ferox, then try trolling.

Feeding Loch Rannoch at its western end is the outflow from Loch Laidon, six miles further west, on Rannoch Moor. Laidon teems with native brown trout, and its shores offer a wealth of attractive bays. Anglers here can expect to catch more than 20, 8–12 oz trout a day. It is an ideal loch for beginners and seasoned anglers alike.

Exploring Rannoch Moor is well worth the effort. Its magical landscape has remained unchanged for thousands of years. The water-logged peat is about 20 ft deep, and the wettest areas are sprinkled with tufts of cotton grass bobbing in the breeze. Coarse sedges cling to drier hummocks and provide shelter for red grouse, merlin, snipe and curlew.

Rannoch is one of the Scotland's last remaining secrets. Its landscape is jewelled with golden spikes of bog asphodel, coral-shaped lichens and sweet-scented bog-myrtle. The only decision an angler faces is whether to explore the moor or the loch first. It's a dilemma which is often resolved by the ring of a rising trout.

L OCH RANNOCH. This silvery expanse of water holds wild brown trout of 12 oz around shallower margins. But in deeper areas lurk ferox of unknown size. There could be one with your name on. If Rannoch is dour then explore the surrounding wilderness of moors.

15. The Northeast and Moray

The Findhorn

LOCATION: Ordnance Survey Land Ranger Series, 1:50,000. Sheets 35, Kingussie; and 27, Nairn.

GRID REFERENCES: Sheet 35, Tomatin, 806288. **Sheet 27**, Drynachan Lodge, 865395; Randolph's Leap, 998495; Forres, 034587.

SEASONS: Salmon – February 11–September 30, with best fishing in August and September. Lower Findhorn is good in the spring. Trout – April 1–September 30, with May and June best.

FLIES: Salmon – Munro Killer, Stoat's Tail, Black Doctor, Garry Dog, Stuart's Killer. Trout – Various Butchers, Black Pennell, Greenwell's Glory.

COSTS: Many beats are booked year after year by the same rods. However, some fishing is available on certain estates. Expect to pay anything from £7.50 per rod a day up at Tomatin to £70 per rod per day further downstream. Drynachan Fishings cost £57.50 per rod a day, plus £250 per week for the use of the estate cottage, which sleeps six. The best month here is September.

PERMISSION: Tomatin:
Freeburn Hotel, Tomatin, Inverness
(Tel: 08082–205).
Cawdor Estate: Cawdor Estates Office, Cawdor, Nairn (Tel 0667–666).
Forres Association Water: J Mitchell, The Tackles Shop, High Street, Forres, Morayshire (Tel: 03090–72936).

DANCING, DASHING FINDHORN is a delightful river to fish. Its best angling water lies above Randolph's Leap. Below here, pools do yield, but lack the splendour of the upper beats. The banks are largely strangled by conifer plantations, which give the river a dismal air.

The Findhorn's headwaters lie in the grey Monadhliath Mountains. Its two main tributaries are the boiling, peaty Eskin, and the cascading, crystal Abhainn Cro Chlach. These two burns tumble together to form the Findhorn, proper, and their combined waters are swollen by many streams charging down narrow gullies off the surrounding mountains. The upper reaches are good spawning grounds.

Like many other Scottish rivers, the Findhorn relies on snowmelt to keep its waters fresh and fishable. Mild winters and dry summers leave it looking more like a stream than a formidable salmon river. But given a fast melt in the hills, or a heavy downpour, no other river in the land can rise as quickly. If you wade or fish a narrow part of Findhorn, beware!

Beats of the Findhorn from source to sea are: Coignafearn, Dalmigavie Estates, Clune Estate, Glenmazeran, Glenkyllachy, Corryburgh Estates, Moy Estate, Cawdor Estate, Lethen Estate, Culmony Estate, Glenferness Estate, Dunphail, Estae, Logie Estate, Moray Estates Development Company, and Forres Angling Association water.

Sea-trout can be caught in Findhorn Bay, but in the saltwater they are still soft-mouthed and harder to keep on.

Above Tomatin, anglers come mainly in search of brown trout. Salmon that make it this far are usually in full spawning dress. But exquisite pleasure is to be had from setting out on foot and stalking the upper river in search of brown trout. A day in the mountains may be exhausting, but the reward could be a trout weighing more than 3 lb.

Two miles north of the little highland village of Tomatin, the Findhorn is met by Funtack Burn, which flows first as Moy Burn into Loch Moy before changing its name. Much of the loch is edged by dreaded conifers.

THE DESOLATE MOORLANDS

The little island of Eilean Clach used to have a gallows, no doubt extensively used by the occupants of the castle on the neighbouring island. A large boulder that lies here used to have prisoners chained to it. Castle Moy was built in the late 1300s, but has been deserted since 1655.

From the confluence of Funtack Burn, the Findhorn, winds its way north through a wilderness of heather and scree-strewn mountains. Along this stretch are the famous Drynachan Fishings of Cawdor Estate. The three beats have 35 pools, the most productive being Ballaggan, Red Rock, Boat or Bridge Pool, Carnoch Stream, Corbie, Red Burn, Little Banchor Stream, The Grave, Cow, Big Rock stream and March stream. The five-year average for each of the three beats is 89, 114 and 122 salmon. Accommodation is in a converted gardener's cottage, ideally situated on the bank.

From here, Findhorn weaves its way to the spectacular wooded gorge that makes this river

RIVER FINDHORN. Famous Randolph's Leap. Here the grey limestone rocks are time worn by the relentless waters of the river. It is one of the best places to come to watch returning fish leaping the falls in an attempt to get to their spawning grounds.

The North Esk

one of the most beautiful in Scotland. For more than 18 miles it hurries through a steep pass, waters plunging over dazzling-white quartz rock, thundering through the gorge, in a succession of rapids and black pools. Nowhere can the salmon's strength be better appreciated; or the relentless power of the water when you see enormous granite rocks with holes worn through them.

The most famous part of this spectacular gorge is Randolph's Leap. It was here that Alastair Ban Comyn, Cumming of Dunphail, leapt across the Findhorn with the Comyn Standard to escape execution by Randolph, Earl of Moray. Perhaps this is where pole-vaulting originated. By the Leap a stone marks the level reached by the river in the great flood of 1829. According to one story, a gardener at Relugas caught a salmon with his umbrella, the water being 50 ft above it normal. Eventually, the gorge sides give way to woodlands of oak, beech, birch, rowan and Scots pines and alder. The gorge also acts as a series of temperature holding pools for salmon.

Findhorn salmon average around 10 lb, with fish of 20 lb and more not uncommon. In 1989 Jim Mitchell took one 26 lb from Meads Beat. Sea-trout are also caught. But for true Findhorn fishing, make for the gorge and the desolate moorlands above.

LOCATION: Ordnance Survey Land Ranger Series, 1:50,000. Sheets 44, Ballater, and 45, Stonehaven.

GRID REFERENCES: Sheet 44, Loch Lee, 420795; Water of Mark and Lee Junction 448803; Craigoshina, 573762. **Sheet 45,** Edzell, 605690; Junction Pool 624661; Balmakewan, 665662; Morphie Dyke, 709631.

SEASONS: Salmon – February 16–October 31, with spring and autumn best. Summer sees the river become a trickle. Trout – March 15–October 6, with April, May and June the best months.

FLIES: Salmon – Stoat's Tail, Blue Charm, Shrimp, Hairy Mary, Thunder and Lightning. Trout – March Brown, Greenwell's Glory.

LURES: Brown-and-gold Devon, Yellow-belly, Black-and-Gold.

COSTS: A day's salmon and sea-trout fishing on North Esk will cost from £6 per rod a day in summer, £15–£20 a day in spring, and £25 in autumn. It is excellent value-for-money.

PERMISSION: Canterlands, Gallery and other beats: J Johnston and Sons Ltd, Salmon Fishers, 3 America Street, Montrose, Angus (Tel: 0674-73535).
Burn Loups, Gannochy Gorge: Controller, The Burn House, Glenesk, Edzell, Forfar (Tel 03564-281).
The Burn: Mr R Burnett, Gamekeeper, Sandhill Cottage, Burn Cottage, Edzell, Forfar (Tel: 03564-505).
Gannochy Estate: Mr Ramage, Head Keeper, Gannochy Estate, Edzell, Forfar (Tel: 03564-7331).
Craigo: Montrose Angling Club, Mr G Luke, 3 Meriden Street, Montrose, Angus (Tel: 0674-73535).

TUMBLING NORTH ESK begins life at the confluence of the Water of Lee and Water of Mark, just below Invermark Castle. The castle tower dates from 1526. It was once the stronghold of the Litchsome Lindsays.

The water of Lee flows from Loch Lee and the Water of Mark drains the high, rolling mountains of Glen Mark. The Ladder Burn, tributary of Mark, tumbles from Mount Keen (939 m), most easterly of the Munro mountains. Glen Mark was honoured with a visit from Queen Victoria.

The North Esk flows east from here along the wide floor of Glen Esk, its sides awash with heather, creeping forestry plantations, and woods of silver birch and red-berried rowan. Eventually, its waters, bubbling over gravel beds, emerge from the glen between the Hill of Edzell (228 m) and Manach (265 m).

Craigoshina Waters gave one angler a 13 lb salmon to the fly in 1989. How the fish had made it this far in drought conditions is difficult to surmise. Above Craigoshina, at Millden, is a salmon hatchery, fry from which are planted out each year in the Esk's tributaries. Salmon are also trapped and stripped down at Kinnaber, near the estuary, and their ova planted out in Esk spawning grounds.

The entrance to Glen Esk is guarded by Edzell Castle, built by the Lindsays in the late sixteenth century. One ancestor, Sir David Lindsay, established the beautiful gardens here of precisely-clipped box hedges and rambling roses. From here to the estuary the river runs through

RIVER NORTH ESK. Looking downstream from Marykirk road bridge. There are queues to get onto some of the beats on this spate river, well worth joining and if conditions are right you will have a day to remember.

fertile plains. Its bed is of orange sandstone, littered with gravel and its pools are long and streamy. Wading must be undertaken with care, as the bed shelves in places.

Most stretches of the North Esk Waters are accessible to salmon and sea-trout following improvements by the North Esk District Fishery Board. Obstacles have been blasted away and pools cleared. Only Burn Loups, above Edzell, now halt the passage of fish in low water. Most salmon on Burn Waters are taken by spinning. It is a difficult stretch to fish.

JOIN THE QUEUE

Salmon fishing is best from opening day until May and again in September and October. The average weight of fish is about 9 lb, with 20-pounders not unknown. Good summer runs of grilse come through, water levels permitting, and sea-trout begin moving in from May through to August, and in mild springs, they have been seen in April. The sea-trout average about 2 lb.

UDN still rears its ugly head in the North Esk, and 1989 saw quite a few diseased fish in the river. We must hope that strict monitoring of the situation by the Department of Agriculture and Fisheries will gradually see the end of the disease. As on most rivers, it is worse in dry spells than in wet.

From the bottom of the Burn Waters, North Esk flows through Gannochy with its deep pots. Opening day of 1989 saw Mr Leatherbarrow take a 10 lb fresh-run salmon from Big Gannochy. Following on are Arnhall, Dalladies and Edzell, where the tributary West Water is drawn in at the famous Junction Pool. Many sea-trout and salmon are taken here, and West Water is the most important of the river's feeders with good spawning areas. Fish spawn also in other feeders and in upper reaches of the main river.

Below Edzell are Strachthro, Inglismaldie, Pert, Balmakewan, Gallery, Hatton, Kirktonhill, Canterland and finally Craigo. Some of these lower stretches are excellent fly waters. On Gallery in autumn 1988, Peter Lyons took a 20 lb salmon, and the same period saw more than 20 fish caught there, with weights of 5 lb to 21 lb 8 oz. In 1989, at Morphie, on Canterland, Ian Graham took a 21 lb salmon, but the previous year a lady angler had one of 24 lb.

One other major tributary, Luther Water, feeds North Esk before it reaches Montrose Bay. Its waters are taken in on Balmakewan, and it is another important spawning tributary.

Salmon and sea-trout are netted from the fish-counter above Morphie Dyke, to the tidal reaches, with Stake-nets along the coast. Two netting stations, at Johnshaven and Lunan Water, have been temporarily closed by their operators, Johnstons and Sons, of Montrose. Lets hope others follow suit, but on a permanent basis.

Fishing is quite difficult to come by on the North Esk. Beats are booked year after year by the same rods, or are totally private. However, it is worth joining the queue. A week's fishing here in spring or autumn is worth having, but remember to do a rain-dance before you go.

The South Esk

LOCATION: Ordnance Survey Land Ranger Series, 1:50,000. Sheets 44, Ballater, and, 54, Dundee.

GRID REFERENCES: Sheet 44, Caenlochan National Nature Reserve, 215777; Clova, 326732. **Sheet 54**, Prosen and Esk confluence, 408584; Kintrochat Water, 567588; Kinnaird Dyke, 626583; House of Dun Water, 665585; Montrose Basin, 695580.

SEASONS: Salmon – February 16–October 31. The best time is in autumn, but excellent sport can be had below the dam in June, July and August. Trout – March 15–October 6, with May, June and July best.

FLIES: Salmon – Garry Dog, Hairy Mary, Stoat's Tail, Munro Killer, Thunder and Lightning, Blue Charm. Trout – Peter Ross, Invicta, Teal, Blue and Silver, Soldier Palmer, March Brown.

COSTS: A week's fishing can cost up to £150 per rod, depending on the time of season and the beat. Some fishing around Brechin is available at £5.75 per rod per day, depending on the time of season.

PERMISSION: Kirriemuir: Kirriemuir Angling Club, 13 Clova Road, Kirriemuir, Angus (Tel: 0575–73456).
House of Dun: Mrs J Philips, Broomlee House, by Montrose, Angus (Tel 066481–202).
Justinhaugh: Justinhaugh Hotel, Justinhaugh, by Forfar, Angus (Tel: 030786–257).
Glen Clova: Clova Hotel, Glen Clova, by Kirriemuir, Angus (Tel: 05755–222).
Finavon Castle: Savills, 12 Clerk Street, Brechin, Angus (Tel: 03562–2187)
Kintrockat: Mr Sandeman, East Kintrockat, Brechin, Angus (Tel: 03562–2739).

THE FEEDER BURNS of the South Esk rise high in the mountains of the Caenlochan Nature Reserve. Sweeping down grassy gullies studded with boulders, they gather to form the main river at the head of Glen Clova.

This glen has a salmon hatchery, and each year salmon are trapped and stripped and their eggs hatched. The fry are then planted out in the wealth of excellent feeder burns and in the main river.

South Esk twists and tumbles down the glen over a sandy bed, but waters slow as they leave the glen, and much of the river's remaining course is susceptible to flooding.

Just beyond Cortachy Castle, the main river takes in Prosen Water. Salmon fishing can be especially productive here in autumn months, but the river has excellent fishings from here down to Montrose Careston, Kintrockat, Finavon, Kinnarid and House of Dun. Beats such as Kinnaird are booked years in advance, and are extremely hard to obtain.

RISING AFTER RAIN

One of the Esk's best stretches is the Finavon Castle Water. It is divided into three beats, Castle, Indies, and Meadows and Balgarrock, with more than 30 pools and lies. The 1988 catch was 159 salmon and 308 sea-trout, the salmon averaging about 11 lb.

Kinnaird has a dyke which acts as a temperature barrier to ascending fish in spring. It also has two particularly good pools Arn Pool and Bolster Pool. In March, 1989, salmon of more than 20 lb came from them. The biggest Esk fish was caught in October 1922. It weighed 59 lb and must have given its captor, Mr J K Somerville, the fight of a lifetime.

Esk sea-trout average about 2½ lb, but fish of up to 6 lb are taken each season. Evening outings are sometimes rewarded with four or five fish. Colinshaugh Pool, on Lower Careston, is good, and June and July are the best months.

As the Esk is a spate river, and has no feeder lochs, it depends heavily on spring snowmelt to keep it fishable. Dry summers see its waters become stagnant and weedy, and fishing is best when the river is rising after rain.

Although the lower reaches of Esk are 'lazy', they have a wealth of good pools and lies. Bank fishing can be quite difficult because of the number of trees, but it is well worth perservering.

The South Esk finishes its journey in Montrose Basin, a huge tidal area of silt, mud and marsh.

RIVER SOUTH ESK. From its torrid mountain beginnings the river ends life flowing slowly through gentle pastures with wooded banks before spilling into Montrose Basin. The biggest salmon from this river weighed 59 lb. There well may be another.

The Deveron

LOCATION: Ordnance Survey Land Ranger Series, 1:50,000. Sheets 37, Strathdon; 28, Elgin and 29, Banff.

GRID REFERENCES: Sheet 37, Cabrach, 386268; Black Water Deveron Junction, 382307. **Sheet 28**, Hill of Dumeath, 420376. **Sheet 29**, Bogie/Deveron Junction, 539413; Avochie House, 534466; Miltown Weir, 547482; Mains of Mayen, 575477; Laithers House, 670488, Turriff, 710500; Mountblairy, 691545; Montcoffer, 678613.

SEASONS: Salmon – February 11–October 31, with September and October best. Trout – March 15–September 30, with best fishing in April and May.

FLIES: Salmon – Black Doctor, Silver Stoat's Tail, Munro Killer, Garry Dog. Trout – March Brown, Greenwell's Glory, Black Pennell, Grouse and Claret, Teal and Green.

LURES: Blue-and-silver Devon, Black-and-gold Devon.

COSTS: One week's salmon and sea-trout fishing will cost up to £200 per rod on some of the private beats. A week's salmon, sea-trout and brown trout fishing on Turriff Angling Association water will cost £35 per rod for five days, but is available only to visitors staying in the area.

PERMISSION: Huntly: Castle Hotel, Huntly, Aberdeenshire (Tel: 0466–2696).
Huntly Angling Association Water, including Bogie and Isla: J Christie, 27 Duke Street, Huntly, Aberdeenshire (Tel 0466–2991).
Rothiemay and Mayen: Forbes Arms Hotel, Milltown of Rothiemay, Huntly, Aberdeenshire (Tel: 046681–248).
Mayen: R K Mann, Eadsbush, Steal, Hexham, Northumberland (Tel: 0434–673208).
Avochie: Mr A Coombs, The Salmon Pool and Stream Limited, Lochloy House, Nairn (Tel: 0667–55355).
Mountblairy: Mr A G Morison, Mountblairy Estate, Alvah, Banff (Tel: 02616–250).

su05Angling Association: I Masson, The Cross, 6 Castle Street, Turriff, Aberdeenshire (Tel: 0888–62428).
Banff: Jay-Tee, Sport's Shop, Low Street, Banff (Tel: 02612–5821).
Banff: County Hotel, High Street, Banff (Tel: 02612–5353).

FISHING ON THE Deveron is the realisation of many anglers' dreams. This delightful spate river begins its seaward journey from sparkling burns collecting together at the foot of Hill of Three Stanes (629 m), Alt Sowan (568 m), Creag an Sgor (633 m), Sand Hill (548 m) and the dominating Buck of Cabrach (731 m). It is a place of windswept mountains, carpeted with heather and golden sedges.

The rivers bustling course draws in many tumbling burns, for the principal tributaries are Black Water, the Bogie and the Isla. The Black Water and the upper reaches of the main river are good spawning areas.

From its source, the Deveron flows to Cabrach village where it charges north, squeezed between the steep banks of Daugh of Corinacy and Meikle Firbriggs (539 m). As it dashes from this gorge, Bank of Corinacy, it is joined by Black Water's swirling current. This first beat of Deveron is Cabrach Lodge.

Its waters now swollen, the river flows through Glenfiddich Lodge Beat, Lesmurdie and Beldorney. The last lies at the foot of the wooded Hill of Dumeath (322 m). From Dumeath's other side boils the Burn of Edinglassie.

Beats before the Huntly Angling Association water are Edinglassie and Invermarkie. Although some salmon are caught in these upper reaches, it is brown trout which are the real attraction. Late April, May and September are the best months, and fish of more than 3 lb are not uncommon. Recent years have seen also the capture of occasional rainbow trout, escapees from two fish-farms on the river.

Huntly is the start of magnificent salmon fishing. Year after year these lower beats produce salmon and sea-trout of glass-case size, with occasional heavy brown trout to surprise – or disappoint? – a salmon angler. Huntly town lies between the confluence of the Deveron and its tributary Bogie.

SPAWNING GROUNDS

The Bogie flows north down Strath Bogie from burns rising beyond Rhynie village. It carries both sea-trout and salmon, and has good spawning grounds in its headwaters.

The next beats on the Deveron are Huntly Lodge, Castle Hotel, Corniehaugh and Avochie, these beats have yielded many salmon weighing between 15 lb and 20 lb in recent seasons. One of the most productive pools is Still Pool on Corniehaugh.

Avochie has recently been offered for timeshare in perpetuity on a weekly basis for four rods, with an option of a futher two rods for 20 years. The beat is about two-and-a-half miles long, mostly double-bank fishing, with 23 named pools. The cost of a week varies from £5,750–£19,550.

RIVER SOUTH ESK. Around the town of Brechin fishing is available to visiting anglers for as little as £5.75 per rod per day. As it is a spate river it is wise to do a rain dance before you go.

This beat had been kept until recently by the owner for his own use. In 1984 only a small part of the lower best was fished, but 107 rod-days gave 20 salmon and six sea-trout. With more rods out, the expected annual catch would be 200 salmon and 200 sea-trout. Accommodation is available in converted Avochie House. A boat and a gillie are available.

Inverisla and Woodsie, Coniecleugh, Rothiemay Castle, Upper Mayen, Mayen House, Redhill and Carronhaugh are the next beats downstream. On the first of them is the confluence of the Deveron with its tributary, Isla. Isla does not take many spawning fish, as access upriver is difficult and its gravels are impacted in many places.

Coniecleugh has a weir which halts the passage of migratory fish upstream when water temperatures are low. Quite a few large fish have been caught here in the last three seasons.

Rothiemay Castle, the adjoining beat, gave Mr Herd a 15 lb salmon in 1987, and in the spring of that year, on February 13, three salmon of 12 lb 8 oz, 9 lb 4 oz and 6 lb 8 oz, were caught – excellent sport from a river no longer famous for its spring runs. Rothiemay's best pool is Sunnybrae, and both it and the Mayen beats are fished by guests at the Forbes Arms Hotel in Milltown of Rothiemay. Another prolific pool on the Forbes Arms' waters is Haickburn, on Mains of Mayen.

Downstream are Glennie, Turtory, Ardmeallie, Church, Boat of Turtory, Marnoch Lodge and Euchrie. On Marnoch, Mr Garden caught a fine 10 lb salmon in 1987 from Falconer's Pool. Other salmon that season included a 12½-pounder to Mr Sutherland and fish of 11 lb

and 9 lb to Mr Wood from Islands and Bridge Pool respectively.

Beats from here down to the estuary include Netherdale, Laithers, Ardmeallie, Carnousie, Muiresk, Forglen, Mountblairy, Dunlugas and Moncrofter, flowing through a gentle wooded valley of fine arable soils. The surrounding hills are low and rounded, covered with heather bracken and sedges.

Netherdale gave Mr Stone a mighty 14 lb sea-trout in 1987. Other notable sea-trout from these beats are two from Mountblairy, of 12 lb 8 oz, caught by Mr Curzon in 1987 and the other, from Boghead, a 14½-pounder to Mr Miller on a size 12 Black Pennell. June and July are the best months for sea-trout, and the fish average 3 lb.

PRAY FOR RAIN

Mountblairy is the most famous stretch of the Deveron. It was here, on October 21, 1924, that Mrs Morrison caught her 61 lb salmon, shattering the river's previous record, of 56 lb, caught by Colonel Scott on October 31, 1920. It is worth noting both the Deveron's and the Tay's record fish have been caught by ladies . . .

More recently, in 1987, Mr Slater took a 24 lb salmon from Mountblairy, Mr Moreland a 17-pounder from Muiresk, Mr Ewen one of 20 lb from Forglen, Mr Nick Anderson a 34-pounder from Montcoffer, and Mr Bradford one of 23 lb from Laithers . . . The list, it seems is endless. The average weight of salmon is 10 lb.

A great deal of the Deveron is available to the public, and at least 1,000 salmon and 1,000 sea-trout are taken each year. A good year will yield 3,000 sea-trout and 2,500 salmon. It is a delightful river to fish, but it has no feeder lochs,

so pray for rain 'a'for ye go'.

Below Turiff the Deveron is reduced in flow because of abstraction for drinking water, and its lower pools are liable to silt up. But the District Fishery Board is clearing a lot of them. Eventually, between two bustling towns, Banff and Macduff, the Deveron flows over golden sands to mingle with the North Sea.

Bibliography

Trout Lochs of Scotland, B M Sandison, Allen & Unwin.

Where to Fish, D A Orton, Harmsworth Publishing.

The Salmon Rivers of Scotland, Mills & Grasser, Cassel Limited.

The Great Salmon Rivers of Scotland, John Ashley Cooper, Victor Gollancz.

Game Fishing in Scotland, B M Sandison, Mainstream Publishing.

Portrait of the Lothians, Nigel Tranter, Robert Hale.

Portrait of the Border Country, Nigel Tranter, Robert Hale.

Portrait of the Highlands, W Douglas-Simpson, Robert Hale.

Portrait of Perth, Angus & Fife, D Graham-Campbell, Robert Hale.

Portrait of the Moray Firth, Cuthbert Graham, Robert Hale.

Highland Autumn, W R Mitchell, Robert Hale.

A History of the Scottish People 1560–1830, T C Smout, Collins.

The Central Highlands, Ian Finlay, Batsford.

The Edinburgh History of Scotland, Volumes 1–4, Oliver and Boyd.

Scotland For Fishing, Pastime Publications.

The Salmon and Trout Association Magazine.

Salmon Trout and Sea-Trout Magazine.

Trout and Salmon Magazine.

The Scots Magazine.

LOCH CALADAIL. One of the limestone lochs of Durness. The brown trout are of first class quality and fight like demons. A day on Cadadail should yield two or three fish to 1 lb 8 oz and the opportunity to spot the wild flower Mountain Everlasting.

Personal Record

R IVER NAVER. Safely
in the net, a Naver
salmon. The river has a
ten year average of 455
fish. Over the six beats
are fifty named pools. It
is arguably the north of
Scotland's finest salmon
river.

LOCH/RIVER	LOCATION	CATCH	WEIGHT	DATE	TIME	FLY	NOTES

LITTLE RIVER GRUINARD. This tumbling Highland spate stream is a delight of splashing water. It drains the mighty Loch Fionn. Each year salmon and sea-trout make their way up through the foaming waters to gain access to the loch.

THE WEALTH of fishing available to visiting anglers in Sutherland is second to none. No where else can offer such first class brown trout fishing at such excellent value for money.

LOCH/RIVER	LOCATION	CATCH	WEIGHT	DATE	TIME	FLY	NOTES

LOCH/RIVER	LOCATION	CATCH	WEIGHT	DATE	TIME	FLY	NOTES

Index